Cambridge Elements

Elements in Magic
edited by
William Pooley
University of Bristol

CONJURING THE ARAB MAGICIAN

Intercultural Histories of Magic

Gal Sofer
Ben-Gurion University of the Negev

Shaftesbury Road, Cambridge CB2 8EA, United Kingdom

One Liberty Plaza, 20th Floor, New York, NY 10006, USA

477 Williamstown Road, Port Melbourne, VIC 3207, Australia

314–321, 3rd Floor, Plot 3, Splendor Forum, Jasola District Centre, New Delhi – 110025, India

103 Penang Road, #05–06/07, Visioncrest Commercial, Singapore 238467

Cambridge University Press is part of Cambridge University Press & Assessment, a department of the University of Cambridge.

We share the University's mission to contribute to society through the pursuit of education, learning and research at the highest international levels of excellence.

www.cambridge.org
Information on this title: www.cambridge.org/9781009547185

DOI: 10.1017/9781009547192

© Gal Sofer 2025

This publication is in copyright. Subject to statutory exception and to the provisions of relevant collective licensing agreements, no reproduction of any part may take place without the written permission of Cambridge University Press & Assessment.

When citing this work, please include a reference to the DOI 10.1017/9781009547192

First published 2025

A catalogue record for this publication is available from the British Library

A Cataloging-in-Publication data record for this Element is available from the Library of Congress

ISBN 978-1-009-54722-2 Hardback
ISBN 978-1-009-54718-5 Paperback
ISSN 2732-4087 (online)
ISSN 2732-4079 (print)

Cambridge University Press & Assessment has no responsibility for the persistence or accuracy of URLs for external or third-party internet websites referred to in this publication and does not guarantee that any content on such websites is, or will remain, accurate or appropriate.

For EU product safety concerns, contact us at Calle de José Abascal, 56, 1°, 28003 Madrid, Spain, or email eugpsr@cambridge.org

Conjuring the Arab Magician

Intercultural Histories of Magic

Elements in Magic

DOI: 10.1017/9781009547192
First published online: December 2025

Gal Sofer
Ben-Gurion University of the Negev
Author for correspondence: Gal Sofer, gal.sofer1@gmail.com

Abstract: This Element reassesses narratives of intercultural transmission in medieval European magic, highlighting complex processes of compilation and attribution often obscured by broad labels. Following an Introduction that lays out the methodological framework, Section 1 ("The Wise Saracens") explores a medieval Christian magician's depiction of Islam and the figure of the Arab magician, illustrating how authors blended genuine intercultural exchanges with imaginative attributions. Section 2 ("*The Seven Names*") reconsiders a Latin magical text traditionally labeled "Arabic magic," demonstrating that its complex, multicultural components resist any simple claims of a lost Arabic original. Section 3 ("The Almandel Problem") presents another contested text, showing how philological evidence often complicates a linear model of transmission. Finally, this volume offers a complete edition and translation of *The Book of Seven Names*, discussed in Section 2.

Keywords: Arabic magic, *The Book of Seven Names*, Almandel, multicultural magic, medieval magic

© Gal Sofer 2025

ISBNs: 9781009547222 (HB), 9781009547185 (PB), 9781009547192 (OC)
ISSNs: 2732-4087 (online), 2732-4079 (print)

Contents

Introduction — 1

1 The Wise Saracens: Berengar Ganell and His View on Islam — 9

2 *The Seven Names*: Revisiting an "Arabic Magic" Work — 20

3 The *Almandel* Problem: Do We Have to Assume a Lost Source? — 39

Concluding Remarks — 52

Appendix A: *The Book of Seven Names*: Edition — 55

Appendix B: *The Book of Seven Names*: Translation — 64

Bibliography — 73

Introduction

Scholars of the history of science, especially chemistry, will be familiar with the phenomenon illustrated in this Element.[1] I refer here to what they often called the "Geber problem."[2] As part of the grand narrative of the history of science(s), it is well known that Greek sciences were adopted by Arab scientists, who allowed their penetration into the so-called Latin West through Latin authors who translated these scientific works. This chain of transmission is part and parcel of the historiography of science, and while it is undoubtedly a fair description of how Greek and Arabic sciences were transmitted and traveled, it should not stand as an uncontested paradigm when it comes to the examination of certain specific works. The "Geber problem" can be seen as revolving around this specific issue. It expresses the apparent tension between the grand narrative of the scientific works' mode of transmission and the facts that can be extracted from the actual texts.

Geber is the Latin name for Jābir (hence, Geber) ibn Ḥayyān, who is known from several works as an alchemist who was presumably active during the eighth century in Baghdad.[3] When Geber's texts appeared in the Latin West, they were regarded by their readers as translations of Jābir's alchemical works. They were also considered as such by nineteenth-century scholars, who were familiar with the figure of Jābir and his works. Holding the grand narrative of the Greek–Arabic–Latin direction of transmission, it was only reasonable for them to ascribe to Jābir the authorship of Geber's works, arguing that the Geberian corpus is, indeed, a body of translated texts from Arabic into Latin. The fact that the assumed original works, which were supposed to represent Geber's sources, could not be found was attributed to their loss or a yet-to-be-discovered piece of history. All these views were later revised, based on a close reading of the Geberian texts. Today, there is almost a consensus about Geber: not Jābir, and not even an Arab, but an Italian Franciscan friar, who promoted his work by ascribing it to Geber, that is, Jābir, whose status as the historical figure behind Arabic sources that have survived has been contested since then. It is commonly accepted that those sources represent not a single author but

---

[1] I am grateful to the anonymous reviewers whose important comments and suggestions have substantially improved this Element.
[2] The most comprehensive history of this problem, as well as the "solution" for it, was written by William R. Newman in several publications. See, among them, Newman, "New Light on the Identity of 'Geber.'" See also Newman's introduction in Newman, *The Summa Perfectionis*, 57–108. In relation to the (al)chemical texts, see Principe, *The Secrets of Alchemy*, 54–58.
[3] For the identity of Jābir, see Principe, *The Secrets of Alchemy*, 33–35.

a group of Shi'i (sometimes more specifically Ismā'īlī) scholars who were active during the eighth and ninth centuries.[4] The works of Geber were not translations of Arabic texts but rather original pieces by the Italian friar, whose name might also be a pseudonym – Paul of Taranto, presumably a lecturer in Assisi.[5]

The "Geber problem" is much more than an interesting anecdote in the historiography of science. It is a thought-provoking and tantalizing case that calls for our caution and hesitation when describing the texts we are working on. Why and how do we assume that the text in front of us originated in a different cultural or linguistic context? What kind of evidence do we possess that supports our thesis? What is the impact of grand narratives on our philological sense? To what extent can we trust our medieval authors, not in terms of falsehood but in their perception of authority and attribution? These are only some of the questions that the Geber problem poses to historians seeking to understand the development of knowledge within its historical, social, and cultural context. This Element calls for reflection on these questions when interpreting magical texts to better situate them in the history of knowledge transmission.

Earlier generations of scholarship, shaped by Orientalist assumptions, sometimes attributed works to "the Arabs" or posited a lost Arabic source. Consider, for example, the following citation of the late great scholar of Jewish studies Gershom Scholem:

> Nothing in the content of these traditions prevents us from asserting that their origin is in the East … The imagination of the Arabs concerning demons was rich, as is well known, while this is not the case for the imagination of the people of the West in the Middle Ages. These demonological methods, with all their fantasies, result from the winds that blow in the air in which their creators lived; [that is,] in the Eastern air.[6]

Contrary to his assumption, Scholem, writing in the mid twentieth century, lacked a firm basis for positing an "Eastern" origin. The traditions he refers to – attested in anonymous sources used by the medieval thinker Isaac HaKohen – show no signs of a translation process, nor is there any comparable source to suggest such a lineage.[7] "It is very difficult to perceive them as formatted in the West," noted Scholem concerning the

---

[4] See the updated discussion by Ebstein, *Mysticism and Philosophy in al-Andalus*, 30–32.
[5] Newman, *The Summa Perfectionis*, 102–103.
[6] Unless otherwise noted, all translations in this Element are my own. See Scholem, "R. Isaac ben Jacob Hacohen III," 285. On Scholem's Orientalist presuppositions, see Huss, *Mystifying Kabbalah*, 117–123.
[7] On the demonic-magic context of these sources (among them, *The Air of the Demons*), which Isaac mentioned, see Sofer, *Solomonic Magic*, 219–222.

demonological materials, without giving any textual evidence to support his claim, nor citing a related "Eastern" (let alone Arabic) work that might have served as the basis for his argument. Writing about the imagination of the Arabs, as opposed to the ("rationalistic") imagination of the West, Scholem proposed no less imagined connections between the materials that circulated in the West and Arabic demonology – a field with which he was familiar and about which he wrote in other publications.[8]

Even setting aside the lack of textual evidence, Scholem's reasoning reflects an early twentieth-century Orientalist perspective, locating imaginative power in the "East" and explanatory deficiency in the "West."[9] In certain strands of Jewish studies scholarship, such assertions led to a sharp emphasis on Arabic elements, primarily onomastics, as markers of an Arabic textual source. Latin counterparts, on the other hand, have not received such treatment. When Scholem read a magical work with Latin terms, he did not necessarily assume a Latin source behind it and sometimes completely ignored it. That is the case with a late thirteenth-century or early fourteenth-century Hebrew work circulated under the title *Berit Menuḥa* (The Covenant of Serenity). *Berit Menuḥa* is a treatise on divine cosmology and angelology which also contains detailed magical recipes for finding water in the desert, triumphing in war, healing, bringing about an enemy's downfall, and other purposes. In some parts of the work, the names of famous demonic kings – known already from Arabic sources – are listed, after being explicitly described as originating from Arabic sources: "And in Arabic they are called ʾLMWDHB the ruler of Sunday, ʾLḤʾRT – and this is ʾBW MWRʾ – the ruler of Monday, ʾLḤMR the ruler of Tuesday, BRQʾN the ruler of Wednesday, ŠMḤWRYŠ the ruler of Thursday, ʾLʾBYS the ruler of Friday, MYMWN ʾLSḤʾBY the ruler of Saturday, [and] MYMWN son of NḤ rules them all."[10]

While Scholem commented on such appearances of Arabic materials in the text,[11] he completely ignored the preceding words in this list: "Enhance the power of these eight kings who are named Kheshalshun Ḥadlimon Qantefit Tarfit Shadrakh Meishakh ʿAvidinno ʾAlfaʾeiro." Without attempting to clarify all the figures named here, one can readily

---

[8] For example, see Scholem, "Jewish-Arabic Demonology."
[9] On Scholem's attitude toward magic, see Bohak, "Gershom Scholem."
[10] For the original Hebrew, see Porat, *Brit ha-Menuḥa*, 374.
[11] Scholem, "Bilar," 27. On p. 20, Scholem added a reservation yet still preserved the idea of an underlying "pure" text: "Of course, we do not know whether the author of *Berit Menuḥa* drew from Hebrew sources or whether he took all this material directly from Arabic books. It seems that there was another intermediary involved, for the adjurations became mixed with sacred names of purely Jewish origin."

identify the three children from Daniel 1:7 – frequently mentioned in Latin adjurations – by their Aramaic names: Shadrach, Meshach, and Abednego.[12] The last name is also noteworthy as it appears to derive from the Christian phrase "Alpha et O[mega]," which is likewise common in Latin magical sources.[13] In this instance, the working assumption of an Arabic provenance may have diverted attention from the equally significant Latin and Christian resonances, narrowing the analytical lens applied to the text's composite character.

A residual form of this narrow lens, I argue, can still be detected in a few modern scholarly works. For example, a recent critical edition of *Berit Menuḥa*, working closely with Scholem's notes, again invokes the Arabic strata, situating the treatise within broader "Eastern" currents and, via phenomenological rather than philological comparison, juxtaposes certain notions with those of Kashmiri Śaivism.[14] However, all these formulas point to an author who combined various materials into his own system of magic, explicitly equating the Latin names (whether or not he understood them – this remains open to debate) with Arabic ones. This reflects a multicultural environment rather than a specific lost Arabic or Latin urtext.

Scholem's case is an extreme example, and it does not accurately reflect contemporary scholarship.[15] Yet, in studying the history of magic, we sometimes seek out the foreign to pinpoint a (textual) source. The remote origin is sometimes assumed to lie elsewhere, in another language and cultural framework. When it erupts into the text – often in the form of untranslated short formulas or *nomina magica* – we take this as evidence that another original layer, obscured by processes of cultural translation, has now been revealed, resisting efforts to render it into a different linguistic or cultural context. Yet the assumption that scribes were skilled enough to translate most of a text but somehow unable to handle parts of it is more often asserted than demonstrated. When Scholem encountered a Hebrew magical work that included a paragraph in Judeo-Arabic, he concluded

---

[12] For Latin recipes that invoke their names, see, for example, Kieckhefer, *Forbidden Rites*, 252–253.

[13] See Sofer, *Solomonic Magic*, chapter 10.

[14] See the phenomenological discussion in the introduction of Porat, *Brit ha-Menuḥa*.

[15] For example, Hebrew elements that appeared in Arabic sources were less often attributed to a long-lost Hebrew urtext. See, for example, the work of Joaquina Albarracín Navarro and Juan Martínez Ruiz on what they named "the miscellany of Solomon," in which Hebrew words can be found but were not interpreted by the authors as evidence for a lost Hebrew origin. See Albarracín Navarro and Martínez Ruiz, *Medicina*, esp. 35–37.

that this confirmed the work's Arabic origin.[16] But, if this is indeed the case, is it not strange that the scribe could translate some sections but not others that pose no apparent difficulty? In the case in question, it is more plausible that the author inserted the paragraph from another source, rather than being unable – or, as Scholem suggested, simply unwilling – to translate it.[17] In any case, it may be more productive to refrain from assuming our authors' inability to work with a language they otherwise seem able to translate.

Borrowed from classical Lachmannism, close reading of an unexpected passage is sometimes treated as a chance to "catch the thief red-handed" and to sketch a *stemma codicum*. But a sudden "foreign" intrusion is not, by itself, proof of a lost foreign urtext or prototype. More often, it registers an encounter between our expectations and what the manuscript actually transmits. As scholars of magic acknowledge, a Hebrew formula inside a Latin treatise, for instance, need not point to an entire Hebrew original; it simply documents contact – direct or indirect, real or imagined – between Hebrew and Latin textual worlds. Such an encounter may be direct (e.g., an exchange of knowledge between experts, textually and orally) or indirect (e.g., a later borrowing resulting from such an exchange), actual or imagined.[18] Such cross-pollination is typical of learned magic, yielding a richly layered record of transmission and transformation.[19] Consider, for example, the transliterated (Hebrew to Latin) Jewish prayer *Shema Yisrael*, which appears in several magical works written in Latin. Such formulas are striking evidence of intercultural encounters but do not support the idea of a Hebrew urtext. Likewise, the modern Arabic *Sifr Ādam* reveals an equally complex trail of borrowings and adaptations.[20]

The nuance of such a detailed and complex textual transmission, which modern scholarship broadly accepts, can be blurred when we rely on umbrella labels. As modern studies recognize, the use of broad categories such as "Jewish magic" does not convey the idea of a Jewish urtext, but

---

[16] Scholem, "Bilar," 14. Scholem also provided other evidence, such as the appearance of Quranic figures in the texts.
[17] Ibid. On this text and its history, see Sofer, *Solomonic Magic*, chapter 4.
[18] Knowledge exchange between magicians is common but not always recorded as such. For a recorded case in which a magician sought magical knowledge among magicians of the "other," see Martin, *Witchcraft and the Inquisition in Venice: 1550–1650*, 98.
[19] See the fascinating analogy made by Klaassen, in which these texts are likened to Frankenstein's monster. See Klaassen, *The Transformations of Magic*, 115. See also Sofer, *Solomonic Magic*, chapter 1.
[20] Fodor, "An Arabic Version of 'Sefer ha-Razim'"; Fodor, "An Arabic Version of 'The Sword of Moses'"; Zsom, "Another Arabic Version of Sefer ha-Razim and Ḥarba de-Moše: A New Sifr Ādam Manuscript."

rather a very concrete and specific case in which a Jewish scribe engaged with a magical text, whatever this text might include.[21] For that reason, the label "Jewish magic" is best reserved for these cases. Applying the same tag to compilations produced by non-Jewish scribes may inadvertently suggest that the work is inherently "Jewish" or that a Jewish intermediary must lie behind it. The same caution applies to the companion label "Arabic magic." When a text is written in Arabic or demonstrably compiled by an Arabic-speaking author, the descriptor is perfectly transparent: It signals the language of composition and the compiler's milieu, without implying a pristine original. But what exactly are we saying when labeling a Latin text as a work of "Arabic magic"? In what follows, I will use the term "multicultural magic" to refer to compilations that display precisely these layered encounters – texts in which Latin, Arabic, Hebrew, Greek, and other traditions intersect. This term makes it explicit that a foreign element signals contact, not necessarily a hidden, homogeneous urtext.

When considering that a text may have a lost Arabic origin, another aspect should be taken into account. In his famous and forceful critique of what he called "the classical narrative" in the historiography of science, George Saliba has shown how specific details challenge this narrative – namely, the view that the Arabs were merely recipients of Greek science, functioning as passive vessels without original contributions.[22] They were also portrayed as mere transmitters who, in the eyes of European Renaissance scholars, were sometimes considered defective and whose works were to be discarded.[23] Of course, these assumptions are no longer accepted today, and the attitudes of authors and practitioners of magic toward Arabic science (and magic) are taken into account when examining the works that serve as our research sources. Their perception of what they considered "Arabic" is crucial for our study, as we will see later.

It may surprise the reader that this study does not attempt to define, examine, or contribute directly to the field of "Arabic magic." This field has grown considerably over the past decade, enriched by exceptional research grounded in close textual analysis. Recent studies by scholars such as Charles Burnett, Jean-Charles Coulon, Noah Gardiner, Matthew

---

[21] See, for example, Bohak, *Ancient Jewish Magic*, and the many discussions there on Jewish borrowings from non-Jewish sources, esp. 227–290. See also Harari, Jewish Magic, esp. 207–293; Boustan and Sanzo, "Christian Magicians, Jewish Magical Idioms, and the Shared Magical Culture of Late Antiquity."

[22] Saliba, *Islamic Science and the Making of the European Renaissance*.

[23] See, for example, Siraisi, *Avicenna in Renaissance Italy*, 66–76. See also Section 3.

Melvin-Koushki, Liana Saif, Emilie Savage-Smith, Emily Selove, and others have immensely contributed to our understanding of Arabic (Islamic and non-Islamic) magic, as well as the reception of Arabic magic in non-Arabic cultures and "the Latin West."[24] While this Element will be based on this scholarship, we will not discuss the Arabic texts per se in what follows.[25] Instead, this study will center on what we might call "the imagined Arab magician" and how this notion may have shaped our understanding and historiography of certain magical (or scientific) works. Specifically, we will begin by examining how a fourteenth-century Christian magician viewed the Arabic language and Muslim practitioners. In doing so, we will ask whether the magician's efforts to link certain magical practices to Arabs reflect genuine transmission – that is, his having actually learned them from Arab practitioners – or whether these are more a product of his own invention.

After exploring the role of the "imagined Arab magician" – the "magical Geber" – we will turn to a Latin work attributed to an Arabic figure, which scholars have regarded as a text of Arabic origin: *The Seven Names*. Interestingly, one of the first modern scholars to discuss this work, the late David Pingree – an eminent historian of science – was already well aware of the "Geber problem."[26] A closer reading suggests that a lost Arabic original is not necessary to explain the text's features, and presuming one may obscure its complex development, authorship, and context. More critically, it narrows the search for parallels to one cultural zone, when, as in the Geber case, relevant evidence may lie elsewhere.

---

[24] Many studies can be listed here, and I by no means aspire to create an exhaustive list. See, among many others, Bohak and Burnett, *Thābit ibn Qurra*; Burnett, "Arabic Magic"; Burnett, *Magic and Divination in the Middle Ages*; Burnett and Saif, "The Aping of Culinary Recipes in Magical Texts"; Coulon, *La magie en terre d'islam au Moyen Âge*; Gardiner, "Esotericism"; Porter, Saif, and Savage-Smith, "Medieval Islamic Amulets, Talismans, and Magic"; Saif, Leoni, Melvin-Koushki, and Yahya (eds.), *Islamicate Occult Sciences in Theory and Practice*; Saif, *The Arabic Influences on Early Modern Occult Philosophy*; Saif, "The Cows and the Bees"; Savage-Smith (ed.), *Magic and Divination in Early Islam*; Selove, *The Donkey King*. See also the special issue of *Arabica* (64) edited by Melvin-Koushki and Gardiner, *Islamicate Occultism: New Perspectives*. Naturally, numerous other works will be referenced throughout this Element.

[25] For the current state of research on Arabic magic, the readers will be greatly aided by the thorough review of Günther and Pielow's edited volume *Die Geheimnisse der oberen und der unteren Welt* written by Melvin-Koushki in "Magic in Islam between Religion and Science." Several volumes have been published since Melvin-Koushki's review, including, for example, Garcia Probert and Sijpesteijn, *Amulets and Talismans of the Middle East and North Africa in Context*; Mallett, Rider and Agius, *Magic in Malta*; de Callataÿ and Moureau, *Power, Religion, and Wisdom*.

[26] Pingree, "Learned Magic."

In the past, a few influential mid twentieth-century scholars sometimes viewed such texts as products of a single "pure" tradition (for example, by positing an entirely Arabic provenance).[27] When applied uncritically, such an approach can overlook the reality that many medieval works were the result of ongoing intercultural and interreligious exchanges. In the case of *The Seven Names*, assuming an Arabic prototype quickly led to a second assumption: that the prototype entered Latin literature through a specific wave of translations. I do not contest that translation trend, but I suggest that combining these two suppositions risks creating an overly linear story.

We will conclude this Element with an especially challenging case: whether one can or should posit an Arabic origin for a text when the Latin sources clearly preserve traces of Arabic words. Rather than proposing a definitive answer, I offer a different approach. Instead of asking whether the Latin text is based on an original Arabic work, we should consider why Latin authors found an Arabic text suitable for their purposes, the historical context in which such adaptations might have occurred, and the sources available to these authors. This is not an effort to reassert an Arabic origin or resurrect the "imagined Arab magician" and his equally imagined works, but rather to highlight the breadth of intellectual activity generated through direct and indirect intercultural exchanges. Accordingly, this third section will propose another hypothesis regarding the history of the text.

Writing about these cases is difficult. Reexamining the assumptions regarding Arabic sources is no simple task, as it is deeply entangled with Orientalist perspectives and tendencies toward cultural appropriation. At the same time, such a revisiting can be interpreted as minimizing the significance of Arabic texts in shaping European learned magic – an impression I do not intend to convey. Nevertheless, caution is needed when using reductive categories to depict the transmission processes, avoiding overly broad strokes in works that merit more nuanced attention. The following discussion illustrates how sweeping generalizations can sometimes hinder our ability to recognize the more complex – and less stable – histories underlying texts that are sometimes described in terms that may imply, even unwillingly, a single, uniform (or monochromatic) framework. Such histories are inherent to multicultural magic.

---

[27] I have used the word "pure" here as it was used in the past. See, for example, Scholem's comment about "pure Arabic sources" as the origin of specific demonology in Scholem, "Bilar," 20 n. 41. See also the use of the phrase "pure Arabic magic" in ibid., 49.

1 The Wise Saracens: Berengar Ganell and His View on Islam

Berengar Ganell, a fourteenth-century Christian magician from Catalonia, is an important figure in the history of learned magic. This author, who collected and compiled materials from various sources to create his magnum opus, the *Summa Sacre Magice*, composed his work without being anonymous, demonstrating historical awareness, raising questions about the contradictions in the texts, and exhibiting transparency – albeit sometimes illusory – about the strategies of collection and compilation he employed.[28] We also know about his activities as a magician and advisor to other practitioners through legal documents in which he is mentioned, as well as his interactions with anonymous experts presented in his work.[29]

Ganell completed the *Summa Sacre Magice* in 1346, following his stay in Perpignan, where he collected translations of works from Hebrew and Arabic into Latin.[30] The "sacred magic" he developed consciously and explicitly relied on the four languages that dominated the scientific discourse of the time – Latin, Greek, Arabic, and Hebrew – and he even compared his magical system to philosophy. Just as the sciences and the grammar of the philosophers rest on these four languages, he argued, so does magic rely on the same four languages.[31] Considering the fact that Ganell held a specific notion about the chronology of world religions – paganism came first, then Judaism, Christianity, and finally Islam – his comparison of his magic to philosophy draws on that same sense of historical awareness, enabling him to cast himself as a contemporary philosopher.[32] Situating himself in respect to others was important to Ganell, who often did so explicitly. He consistently compared "sects" (what we would call today "religions," broadly speaking) in terms of their sources of power, authority, ability to work through the sacred magic, and the potential efficacy of their magic. In these points, we can learn about Ganell's treatment of foreign sources and his complex approach toward non-Christian practitioners of magic.

---

[28] Ganell, thus, can be seen as an author-magician. On the author-magician, see Weill-Parot, "Cecco d'Ascoli and Antonio da Montolmo"; Weill-Parot, *Les "images astrologiques,"* 602–636.

[29] Baron, "Un procès de magie en Gévaudan et ses enjeux politiques (1347)"; Boudet and Véronèse, "Le secret dans la magie rituelle médiévale," 141–142.

[30] Gehr, "Beringarius Ganellus." On the Hebrew sources Ganell used, see Sofer, "Wearing God."

[31] Sofer, "Wearing God," 307, n. 12.

[32] This is also supported by the fact that texts of learned magic sometimes indeed refer to the practitioner as a philosopher. For example, *Liber Iuratus Honorii*, which was known to Ganell. See Veenstra, "Honorius and the Sigil of God."

While Ganell used Latin sources that, in turn, are based on Hebrew and Arabic works – and by that, I should also specifically state Jewish and Islamic – he had ambivalent sentiments toward non-Christian practitioners. In an attempt to situate himself and his "sect," that is, Catholicism, in world history, he raised questions regarding the antiquity of his own materials, yet was still well aware of the multicultural nature of his sacred magic:

> Also, know that this art, as mentioned above, is founded on four sects. However, since during Solomon's time there was no Christian or Mohammedan sect, it seems impossible for it to have been founded on four sects at that time. On the other hand, this seems necessary because Solomon himself placed on his sacred table, which he worked with, the four alphabets of the four sects, as is evident to those who observe it. Therefore, there remains a great doubt.[33]

Ganell is worried. King Solomon, to whom Ganell attributes many of his sources, lived in a world where no Christian or Islamic practitioners could be found. How, then, can this Solomonic magical art be so multicultural? How could Solomon use the alphabets of the Christian and Mohammedan – that is, the Latin and Arabic alphabets – in a pre-Christian and pre-Islamic world? The tension felt by Ganell here is clear, and he allowed himself to describe this as a "great doubt," a phrase full of hesitation. He later offered a possible solution, which – in the presence of this *magnum dubium* – did not seem to convince him either: The alphabets existed even before the religions associated with them.

Constructing his spells, Ganell used the sources available to him. Thus, he found the Arabic names of the lunar mansions appropriate for certain spells, interweaving them with angelic names he found in other sources. Consider, for example, this part of a long conjuration:

> Also, I conjure, adjure, and compel you, N., to come, appear, and render according to the names of the 28 mansions of the moon: Alnath, Albuthah ... And by the angels dwelling therein, with those 7 front liners [*acierum*], whom I call to my aid by the power of your name, God Eyeassereye, whom I name by their letters: Horpenyel, Tyggara, Danael, Kalamya, Acymor, Paschar, Boel.[34]

---

[33] Kassel, Landesbibliothek und Murhardsche Bibliothek der Stadt Kassel, 4° MS. astron. 3 (henceforth: SSM), 138v: "Item scias quod ars ista ut supradictum est in sectis 4 fundatur. Sed cum tempore Salomonis non esset secta Christiana, nec Machometina, qualiter fundabatur in 4 sectis tunc videtur impossibile. Et aliter videtur necessarium quia ipse met Salomon ponit in sua sacra tabula qua operabatur 4 alphabeta 4 sectarum, ut patet intuenti. Quare restat magnum dubium."

[34] SSM, 19r-v: "Item coniuro, contestor, et violo te, N., venire, apparere et rendere per nomina 28 mansionum lune: Alnath, Albuthah ... Et per angelos in ipsis habitantes,

In a single spell, we can see the use of the Arabic lunar mansions (Alnath and Albuthah being the first ones, النطح and البطين) and the seven Hebrew angelic figures that were known to Ganell through *Liber Razielis*, the Book of Raziel.[35] The Arabic lunar mansions have long been available in Latin sources, and Ganell needed them to complete his system of magic.[36] Thus, he did not ignore the Arabic sources that he, in fact, could not access without the Latin mediator. It was important to him to mention that the sacred magic is based on languages and sources, even though he could not read them. He knew no Arabic or Hebrew, except for some basics: the direction of writing/reading (that is, from right to left), the alphabet, and a few words, some of which do not necessitate any serious Arabic proficiency whatsoever (e.g., Allah). While he could not read the Arabic and Hebrew sources directly and felt "a great doubt" when he compared his theory of the development of this multicultural magic with his view on world history, he still insisted on incorporating them.

Let us make this case even more complicated: Ganell did not appreciate Jewish or Muslim practitioners, to whom he ascribed some of his sources. In his *Summa*, he attacks Jewish practitioners, whom he accused of acting against God's will and practicing *nigromancy*, as opposed to the Christian practitioners who practiced the perfect sacred magic.[37] While he does not explicitly mention here Jewish practitioners, he refers to them as those who ask God or His name things, as "this art presupposes that God is in His name, and His name is in Him."[38] The presupposition that Ganell refers to is actually a translation of a Hebrew phrase with which he was familiar through a Latin translation.[39]

Both Muslims and Jews, according to Ganell, hold false beliefs, which makes their magic less effective.[40] When describing world religions,

---

cum illis 7 acierum, quos clamo in meum adiutorium in virtute nominis tui, deus Eyeassereye, quos nomino per suas litteras: Horpenyel, Tyggara, Danael, Kalamya, Acymor, Paschar, Boel."

[35] On the use of the lunar mansions in different astrological genres, see Burnett, "Lunar Astrology"; Samsó, "Lunar Mansions."

[36] Ganell probably had access to this knowledge through the Latin *Picatrix*, a translation and rework of the Arabic *Ghāyat Al-Ḥakīm*. For a recent study and translation, see Attrell and Porreca, *Picatrix*.

[37] On Ganell's distinction between the Christian (new) magical art and the Jewish (old) one, see Gehr, "Beringarius Ganellus," 244.

[38] SSM, 60v: "Cum ars hec presuponat quod Deus est in suo nomine, et nomen suum in eo."

[39] I refer here to *Shi'ur Qomah*. On this phrase in *Shi'ur Qomah*, see Idel, "The Concept of the Torah," 52. On the acquaintance of Ganell with *Shi'ur Qomah*, see Sofer, "Wearing God."

[40] Interestingly, archbishop Rodrigo Jiménez de Rada (1170–1247) narrated the formative story of Islam starting from Muhammad's fall into the deception of a Jewish magician. See Pick, *Conflict and Coexistence*, 77–79.

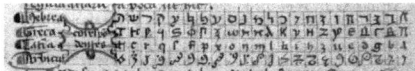

Figure 1 Alphabets correspondences (Kassel, Landesbibliothek und Murhardsche Bibliothek der Stadt Kassel, 4° MS. astron. 3, 131v).

he criticizes both Jews (for not believing in the Trinity) and Muslims (for following Muḥammad):

> And of these religions, the first was paganism, which worshipped the planets and called them gods ... The second was the Hebrew [religion]. And these [Hebrews] believe in one true God, but not that He is triune. The third is Christianity, which confesses the Trinity and the unity. The fourth is the Mohammedan [religion], which, despite believing in God, still believes the scoundrel (*ribaldum*) Muḥammad to be a prophet of God.[41]

None of these harsh words brought Ganell to the conclusion that Hebrew and Arabic sources – which he identified as Jewish and Islamic, respectively – are useless or fraudulent. As practitioners, their magic is less effective. But they are great as transmitters of knowledge, which goes back to (at least) King Solomon. Furthermore, the Hebrew and Arabic alphabets played an important role in Ganell's system of magic, as noted, and the equation between them is made explicitly in the *Summa*. One only needs to observe his alphabetic tables to see how Ganell perceived them as comparable (Figure 1).

While Ganell did not appreciate the beliefs of the Jews or the Muslims, he did not treat their magic at the same level. I suggest that his comparison of the sacred magic to "the grammar of the philosophers" is highly revealing in that context: Ganell wanted his sacred magic to be seen as transmitted through the same channels. We have already seen his historical awareness and how he situated his magic within a religious framework, while also considering world history. It should not surprise us that he was also aware of the transmission of scientific knowledge by Christian scientists (that is, philosophers), some of whose works he evidently used. For example, he drew from Ptolemy's *Quadripartitum* to explain some basic astronomical concepts for those who could not access institutional education: "Therefore, you should at least learn the principles of astrology when you want to involve yourself with magic. But if you do not find a school of astrology,

---

[41] SSM, ff. 117v–118r: "Et de istis sectis prima fuit Hetnica, qua colebat planetas et eos deos vocabat ... Secunda fuit Hebrea. Et isti unum verum Deum credunt, sed non esse trinum. Tercia est Christiana, que trinum et unum confitetur. Quarta est Machometina, que, licet credat Deum, tamen credit ribaldum esse prophetam Dei."

at least know these few rudiments that I will tell you."⁴² He then describes the cosmos with its immovable (empyrean and crystalline) and movable heavens and offers explanations on several topics, including, for example, the various houses and their characteristics, the astrological faces, and the exaltations of the planets. Interestingly, the most popular Latin translation of the Ptolemaic work was made in the same court in which other works possessed by Ganell were made – Alfonso X's court.⁴³ That is to say, Ganell was well aware of the philosophers who granted him access to the knowledge he deemed part of his system of magic, and he had the clear motivation to make his magic appear as (at least partially) their product.

With this in mind, let us examine an interesting case that appears in the fifth book of his *Summa*, in which he copied – but also reworked extensively – a series of recipes from different sources, under the fifth chapter that he entitled "On the art of enchanting and disenchanting" (*De Arte incantandi et disincantandi*).⁴⁴ Ganell presents several recipes there, sometimes explicitly referring to the sources, even in cases where he reworked them. For example, he referred to *Liber Saturni* (the book of Saturn) as the source of some recipes for creating astrological images. *Liber Saturni* is a treatise that was famous during the Middle Ages and early modern period, circulating with other treatises that together were known as *Liber septem planetarum ex scientia Abel*.⁴⁵ The following recipes in the list, although formulated similarly to those of the *Liber Saturni*, are not from this work. Like the recipes of the *Liber Saturni*, they also require the magician to prepare an image at a precise and detailed astrological time. However, on this image, we can find names that are not found in *Liber Saturni*, such as the "seal of the air" that needs to be engraved on the back of the image. This seal is essentially a formula that originated from another work held by Ganell – *Liber Iuratus Honorii* (The Sworn Book of Honorius). It also had an important role in Ganell's *Summa* and subsequently found expression in the astro-magical practices that Ganell developed.⁴⁶

The last recipe in this part is most interesting for us since it reveals how Ganell ascribes texts to different authors or practitioners. This recipe, as

---

[42] SSM, ff. 122r–122v: "Ideo tu addiscas ad minus principia astrologie, quando de magica te volueris intromittere. Sed si non invenis scolam astrologie, saltem scias ista pauca rudimenta que tibi dicam."
[43] The translation was made around 1275 by Egidio de' Tebaldi of Parma. See Boudet, *Entre science et nigromance*, 52.
[44] SSM, 140v–143r.
[45] On this work, see Lucentini and Perrone Compagni, *I testi e i codici*, 66–68; Perrone Compagni, "Studiosus incantationibus," 40–43.
[46] See above, n. 32. On the "seal of the air" formula, see Sofer, "*Ydea Salomonis*," 166–169.

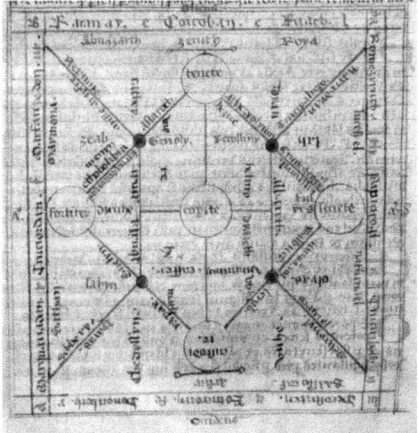

Figure 2 *ad omnia incantanda* (Kassel, Landesbibliothek und Murhardsche Bibliothek der Stadt Kassel, 4° MS. astron. 3, 142v).

mentioned, is part of a series of recipes that mainly discuss astrological images, with some explicit references. However, this method is different, based not on *Liber Saturni* or other known manuals on astrological images. According to Ganell, this is a method for enchanting everything (*ad omnia incantanda*):

> Make the following figure [Figure 2] in any metal and place it over the cause while reading the following words. Therefore, when you have made this figure, you will encircle your cause or a person with it. And, in the center, burying [it] from above or below while saying: "O spirits and demons, masters and barons, fathers of principal malice, powerful, secret, and universal. I conjure you by the power of the Creator and by his secret deeds and words, by the sun and the moon, and by all the lunar bodies of the sky, you, who are sealing the parts by the seal of Sememphorash that dominates over you. By Yaua Eyeassereye Saday Annora Theos Eloy Alla El On, our God (*deus*). Whenever you whom I have sealed over this matter in this seal of such metal, I command you, whenever you seal this matter, compel, preserve, and strongly guard [it], remembering your names thus." In the circle of the world [say]:[47] "Sathan, Maymona, Zeab, Abnalaamar, Amtanasfar, Amnazart, Roya, Lucefyel." In the East: "Rachanay, Corcoban, Rahach." ... [And] Nine times toward all the parts: "Baassocaf, Lucifer, Bethala, Beelzebub. Carry out the command, servants of God Adonai. For I, N., commend you under a pledge to keep this N. and to enchant [it] so that by itself, nor through another, nor through any of the creatures that are under the sky, can it be removed from this place."[48]

---

[47] While this phrase is a bit odd ("in giro saeculi"), it probably refers to the encircling of the object, when it is on the ground (in contrast with "gyro caeli," the circle or sphere of heavens).

[48] SSM, 142r–v.

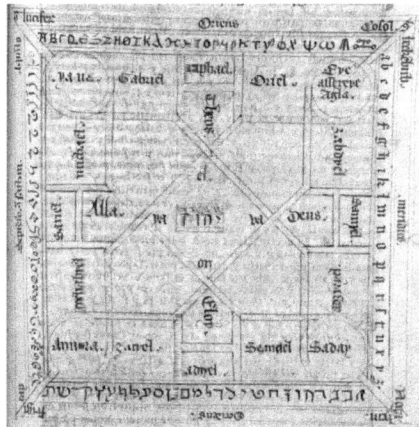

Figure 3 *Tabula Semamephoras* (Kassel, Landesbibliothek und Murhardsche Bibliothek der Stadt Kassel, 4° MS. astron. 3, 38r).

Here we witness a kind of magical recipe that aims to harness the power of spiritual entities to protect, compel, or guard a particular object or person. This procedure starts with the creation of a specific figure, crafted from any metal, which is then placed over (or under) the object or person it is meant to influence. Once the figure is positioned, the practitioner encircles the intended object with the metal figure. The practice involves a series of invocations and names of spirits and demons, calling upon entities across different cardinal directions. In each direction on the figure, there are specific names of spirits that the practitioner commands to bind and guard the object. The names vary from recognizable ones, such as "Lucifer" and "Beelzebub," to less familiar ones. Finally, the practitioner seals the ritual by repeating a command nine times, directing it toward all parts of the world.

The recipe is full of interesting elements, but since our discussion here has revolved around Arabic sources and the attribution of magical knowledge to the Arabs, our focus will be on such markers of multicultural magic. First and foremost, one can easily observe how important it was for Ganell to mention the names of God in all four languages of magic: Greek (Theos), Hebrew (Eloy), Arabic (Alla), and Latin (Deus). This is a hallmark of Ganell's system of magic, and he created a whole *Tabula* that expresses the idea that the four languages of magic, through these godly names, drew their power from the tetragrammaton (Figure 3). The spatial aspect of the *Tabula* was also used in this magical figure, which – as the *Tabula* – is not a magical circle (in which we expect to find the labels that signify the four cardinal directions), but an instrument. For all these reasons, the shaping of the whole figure is undoubtedly of his own pen, as well as the formula "By Yaua Eyeassereye Saday Annora Theos Eloy Alla El On, our God"; this is Ganell's signature.

Yet we can find several names in the recipe that seemingly derive from non-Latin, and even specifically Arabic, sources. Consider, for example, the names "Maymona, Zeab, Abnalaamar, Amtanasfar," which correspond at least partially with Arabic demonological knowledge that existed before the fourteenth century, in which demonic kings are often named after colors.[49] I refer here to the demons Maymūn (ميمون), al-Madhab (المذهب, possibly through the Hebrew *zahav*, transliterated as *Zeab*), ibn al-Aḥmar (ابن الأحمر), and possibly a lesser-known ibn al-Aṣfar (ابن الأصفر). Relying on these Arabic names, one can see why Ganell attributed this recipe to none other than the wise Saracens: "Alternative [method], a most skilled work for enchanting everything, which was used extensively by philosophers and wise Saracens."[50] As mentioned earlier, Ganell tried to posit his magic among the contemporaneous philosophers' knowledge. The attribution of this recipe to the Saracens – a pejorative for Arab Muslims during the Middle Ages – seems to be derived from the same motivation.[51]

The reader who comes across the attribution of this recipe to the Saracens might believe it is genuine; perhaps Ganell somehow met with Muslims who helped him develop his practice, a possibility that should not be ruled out. He, after all, does not seem to use "Saracens" as a pejorative, and in this specific case he described them as wise (*Sarraceni sapientes*). However, as we have already seen, at least one formula in the recipe is his own, and so is the figure's design. Thus, there is no reason to see this attribution as a historical record of an actual encounter. I suggest it is rather an encounter with the imagined Arab magicians, whose knowledge Ganell was eager to access. Interestingly, the Arabic names recorded in this recipe were available to Ganell through a Latin work, an appendix to *Liber Razielis* that he owned. That is, the intercultural encounter here is indirect, mediated by a Latin source. This appendix, *Liber Theysolius*, is attributed to Theyzelius (or Theysolius) the philosopher, who apparently wrote a commentary on *Liber Razielis*.[52] All the Arabic names that Ganell employed were already

---

[49] Consider, for example, the appearance of some of these demonic kings (Maymūn and al-Aḥmar, but possibly also al-Madhab) in an incantation studied by Abbas Ali, "Casting Discord: An Unpublished Spell from the Egyptian National Library." On the seven kings, see Canaan, "Decipherment," 83–86; Winkler, *Siegel und Charaktere*, 97–109; Carboni, "Ginn," 99–102.

[50] SSM, 142r: "Aliter opus expertissimum ad omnia incantanda, quo utebantur multum philosophi et Sarraceni sapientes."

[51] On the imaginary Muslim (and Saracen) in art, see Strickland, *Saracens, Demons, and Jews*, esp. 165–192.

[52] On *Liber Theysolius*, see Page, "Liber Theysolius"; Sofer, *Solomonic Magic*, chapter 11.

in *Liber Theysolius*, suggesting that Ganell derived these names from this source to craft his distinctive "Saracen" recipe.

In essence, Ganell concocted an entire recipe but attributed it to imagined philosophers and wise Saracens, whom he perceived as part of his magical-intellectual milieu. These figures are portrayed as reliable and authoritative, and their knowledge is not only trusted but also valued highly. This aligns with the medieval notion among philosophers that truth should be sought in the original language of translated texts, which is often Arabic.[53] Yet Ganell's scribal strategy is by no means new or innovative, and he was probably also inspired by his sources.

Liber Theysolius, as its name suggests, indicates a Greek source. Theysolius the Greek, as already suggested by Gentile and Gilly, is probably an alias of Toz Graecus, who is often mentioned as the source for other Hermetic texts.[54] Yet a closer examination of the contents of *Liber Theysolius* reveals that Greek influence is, in fact, minimal, and the Hermetic and image-magic materials so closely associated with Toz are notably absent.[55] I would therefore argue that this attribution, too, belongs to the type discussed earlier: a deliberate effort to anchor the knowledge within a particular tradition, guided by a sharp awareness of how such knowledge circulated – along with the names and authorities that lent it legitimacy, authorial voice, and stable ground for the emergence of this multicultural magic.

For a modern reader, such shifting attributions can appear like a sleight of hand. Medieval compilers, however, were operating within what Michel Foucault called the *author function*: a device that groups texts, differentiates them from others, and signals the status a discourse should enjoy within its community.[56] For medieval and early modern scholars, as widely acknowledged by modern scholarship, such attributions were necessary navigational aids through a labyrinth full of different works. Attributing texts to well-known figures, or to names that "sound like" nonspecific figures of a specific "kind," as we will see later, enabled practitioners to quickly evaluate the materials in their hands and place them within their own intellectual endeavors.[57] In other words, the *nomen auctoris* acted as a pragmatic tool of "thrift" that channeled the potentially "cancerous and

---

[53] Burnett, "Arabica Veritas."
[54] Gentile and Gilly, *Marsilio Ficino e il ritorno di Ermete Trismegisto*, 231–232; Page, "Liber Theysolius," 45 n. 20.
[55] On the figure of Toz and the works attributed to him, see Ockenström, "The Deviance of Toz."
[56] Foucault, "What Is an Author?"
[57] Consider, for example, the appearance of Ṭumṭum al-Hindi in the *Picatrix*. See Coulon, *La magie en terre d'islam au Moyen Âge*, 104–110.

dangerous proliferation of significations" which Foucault identifies as the motivation for maintaining the author function at all.[58]

Ganell's creation of his *Summa* exemplifies this practice; he referred to it as a *Summa* because it synthesized various stands, aiming to reconcile differences among authorities or propose intermediary solutions.[59] In this context, attributions were more than mere labels; they were vital to the scholarly discourse, acting as markers within the established literary conventions.[60] In Foucault's terms, the names did not pass "from the interior of a discourse to the real and exterior individual who produced it," but remained on the edge of the text, characterizing its mode of being and the conditions under which it should be received.[61] Recognizing this economy of names helps us avoid both anachronistic suspicions of forgery and uncritical acceptance of single-lineage origin stories.

Of course, Ganell was far from being the first medieval author to collect magical texts from different languages, and one of the compositions that most influenced him – that is, the Latin *Liber Razielis* – was precisely this type of compilation. This work – a collection of various texts explicitly combined into a "book" – was created at the request of Alfonso X, king of Castile, whose translation project also included magical texts.[62] In several places in *Liber Razielis* – as well as in the *Picatrix*, another magical work translated at the king's court – we find references to the Arabic and Indian languages, and in the case of the *Picatrix*, occasional mentions of Indian sages. The extent to which these references reflect a historical account or draw on a specific textual tradition remains an open question that still calls for further research. Yet, as Attrell and Porreca noted, such references might as well be read as "an example of a sort of medieval Arabic 'Orientalism,' whereby the Indians are thought to be an inherently more mystical people by virtue of being a distant (but not too distant) 'Other.'"[63]

Given that Ganell was well acquainted with *Liber Razielis* and the *Picatrix*, it is likely that he embraced the rhetorical style of his Latin predecessors. Attributing knowledge to distant and sometimes exotic sages was a literary strategy that not only helped authors disseminate

---

[58] Foucault, "What Is an Author?" 221.
[59] On Ganell's *Summa* as a *summa*, see Gehr, "Beringarius Ganellus," 240–241.
[60] On the dynamic of such conventions, see the paradigm shift concerning Toz Graecus in Ockenström, "The Deviance of Toz."
[61] Foucault, "What Is an Author?" 211.
[62] Most notably, the *Picatrix*, the *Astromagia*, and the *Liber Razielis*. On the *Picatrix*, see n. 36. On the *Astromagia*, see D'Agostino, *Astromagia*. On the *Liber Razielis*, see Leicht, *Astrologumena Judaica*, 187–294.
[63] Attrell and Porreca, *Picatrix*, 289 n. 24.

their works but also positioned them within a wider intellectual discourse. This was the case for Geber, and it equally applies to Ganell's references to the wise Saracens. This would not be the first time Ganell employed such attributions for this purpose. Elsewhere in the *Summa*, we find none other than Rabbi Akiva presented as the authority behind a calculative method – a name Ganell had encountered in *Liber Theysolius*.[64]

Attributing magical texts to distant or legendary figures is a long-standing practice, dating back to antiquity through the medieval and early modern periods.[65] In the early modern period, as in the Middle Ages, such attributions could be linked to stories of recovering lost or stolen wisdom.[66] In other cases, they serve as a tool for drawing boundaries between illicit and licit forms of magic. Consider, for instance, a recipe for summoning omniscient entities that circulated between the fourteenth and sixteenth centuries, and which, in the eighteenth century, was prefaced with a prologue recounting the story of Rabbi Eliezer, who received a book from his father, Isaac:

> And our Rabbi, Isaac, his father, went to wander in the world because he was hard-pressed for money, and he studied in several places in Babylon and Egypt. When he returned to his land, he brought a book known to the sages of Babylon and the knowledgeable sages of Egypt as "Anigryon," which in the Egyptian language means "Book of Hours."[67] Rabbi Eliezer, his son, seeing that his fortune was favorable, began to engage with it, and he prospered with it for many days until one time, his luck turned, and he almost endangered his life and body. Immediately, when the harmful spirits overpowered him, they did not leave him until he swore to them that he would no longer endeavor in this matter, and so he did.[68]

After this risky attempt, Eliezer received a revelation from Elijah the prophet, who revealed to him the secrets of the following recipe, that is, the recipe that circulated for four hundred years before without mentioning

---

[64] SSM, 134v: "Nunc autem tibi narrabo dicta alterius socii qui hurbiaquiva (!) appellatur." On the appearance of Rabbi Akiva in these texts, I wish to discuss this elsewhere in a separate article.

[65] See, for example, Suárez de la Torre, "Pseudepigraphy and Magic"; Dieleman, *Priests, Tongues, and Rites*, 185–284; Torijano, *Solomon the Esoteric King*.

[66] Consider, for example, Lucas de Tuy's accusation that the Arabs had stolen the science of St. Isidore. See Tolan, *Saracens*, 182.

[67] The word "Anigryon" seems to be derived from ἐγχειρίδιον (*enchiridion*, a handbook).

[68] New York, Manfred and Anne Lehmann Foundation, MS. 343,15v:

ורבינו יצחק אביו הלך כשוט בעולם משום דדחיקא ליה מילתא, שנה בכמה מקומות בבבל ובמצרים. כשחזר לארצו הביא ספר עמו והיה ב' שבני חכמי בבל וחכמי מצרים הבקיא ם בו קור[אים]‏ אותו אַנִיגְרִיאוֹן והוא לשון מצרים ס[פר] שעות. והרב ר' אליעזר בנו על כי ראה מזלו עומד התחיל לעסוק בו והרבה ימים היה מצליח בו עד פעם א' איתרע ליה מזליה וכמעט נסתכן בנפשו ובגופו ומיד כששלטו בו המזיקים לא הניחוהו עד שנשבע להם שלא ישתדל בדבר יותר וכן עשה.

this whole story. The function of the Egyptian and Babylonian imagined sages here is quite different from what we have seen. They are here to mark the illicit, or even defective, and risky practice, in contrast to the recipe that the author offers to the reader. They are not less imaginative, as is the revelation of Elijah, who gives the authoritative voice to the recipe.

Attributing a recipe to an "Arab magician" does not, by itself, prove a specifically Arabic source; the name can be a literary tool even when Arabic elements are present. In cases like these, the emerging picture is sometimes complex and ambivalent. Ganell's *Summa* illustrates the ambiguity: He attacks Islam and Judaism yet eagerly borrows Arabic lunar mansions and Hebrew angelic lore, sometimes presenting this appropriation as the recovery of ancient wisdom. He denounces their prophet and accuses them of practicing *nigromancy* in defiance of God but still draws upon what he perceived as their wisdom. This act of appropriation could at times be framed as the recovery of lost or stolen knowledge – though, as Ganell's *Summa* and the "Geber problem" show, this was not always the case.[69] With this in mind – that attributions to Arab sources could function as literary tools for shaping an author's work within particular historical and cultural contexts, and that attitudes toward the "Other" were often layered and shifting – let us turn to a case in which an Arab author is credited as the source of a Latin magical text typically regarded as an "Arabic work."

2 *The Seven Names*: Revisiting an "Arabic Magic" Work

In 1987, the late David Pingree published a programmatic article entitled "The Diffusion of Arabic Magical Texts in Western Europe." In it, Pingree offered a systematic survey of more than fifty Latin manuscripts containing works translated from Arabic before 1300.[70] According to him, these magical texts were transmitted across medieval Europe in several phases.[71] The earliest phase can be traced to the late eleventh century, when a small number of Arabic texts were first translated into Latin in Italy, and from there made their way to France and England by the early twelfth century. During the twelfth century, additional works translated in Spain reached France and England, attracting considerable interest within intellectual circles in Paris, particularly among figures such as

---

[69] For a striking example of a medieval practitioner who saw himself as deliberately plundering foreign knowledge, see Fanger, "Plundering the Egyptian Treasure."
[70] Pingree, "The Diffusion."
[71] On these phases, see also Burnett, "Arabic Magic."

William of Auvergne (d. 1249).[72] The next major phase took place at the court of Alfonso X – a figure we have already encountered – and involved translations from Arabic and Hebrew sources, which spread into Southern France, especially Montpellier. With this article, Pingree established what we might call the "classical narrative" of the diffusion of magical texts.

In another groundbreaking article, Pingree analyzed a fifteenth-century Latin manuscript preserved at the National Library in Florence, building on his previous research. He compared the works contained in this manuscript with the descriptions – often polemical – provided by William of Auvergne and the author of the *Speculum Astronomiae*.[73] According to Pingree, this manuscript represents one of the most complete extant copies of the new magical texts that reached France from Spain, offering scholars like William an opportunity to encounter them. Thus, the descriptions offered by these theologians are regarded as historical evidence for the circulation of these texts. Indeed, the resemblance is striking – down to the sequence of titles mentioned by the critics, namely William and the author of the *Speculum* – and supports Pingree's argument. This alignment reinforces the historical credibility of their descriptions as evidence of the texts' circulation.

Pingree's identification of this Florentine manuscript remains, thus, persuasive. What it does not establish, however, is that every tract the critics saw had followed a linear route from an Arabic original into Latin. This also does not necessarily mean that the texts encountered by these two critics followed precisely the pathways outlined in Pingree's "classical narrative," nor does it attempt to describe the complex transmission process. In the following sections, I will question the assumption that all these texts were translated directly from Arabic into Latin. Instead, I will explore alternative possibilities that view intercultural encounters not simply as exchanges between passive (recipients) and active (creators or transmitters) agents but as dynamic processes that may have shaped these texts already in their formative stages.

The following discussion would not be the first to question the generalized argument. Following studies on specific texts, the conclusions of Pingree's articles were recently revised and updated by Jean-Patrice Boudet, who also pointed to works that Pingree assumed to be Arabic in origin but are probably not (e.g., *De lapidibus*).[74] It is my attempt

---

[72] On William's attitude toward "Solomonic magic," see Pingree, "Learned Magic," 40–41; Boudet, *Entre science et nigromance*, 145–152 and 217–220; Weill-Parot, Les *"images astrologiques,"* 177–179; Thorndike, *Magic*, II, 338–371.
[73] Pingree, "Learned Magic."
[74] Boudet, "The Transmission of Arabic Magic."

here to follow this direction but also to suggest that the imagined Arab magician might have contributed to the articulation of such arguments in the first place. It is essential to state, however, that nothing here challenges Pingree's entire list: Many texts he treated as Arabic derive demonstrably from Arabic exemplars. The discussion that follows concerns only those pieces for which the putative Arabic source is lost, and no internal evidence points to a full, word-for-word translation that can support the use of the "Arabic magic" category to describe the (lost) origin. In such cases, a more complex chain of compilation – spanning Hebrew, Latin, and perhaps Greek inputs – remains a real possibility, and tracing that complexity is the chief purpose of the sections that follow.

Since Pingree's examination of this codex – and Lynn Thorndike's before him[75] – the Florentine manuscript has become well-known among scholars of medieval magic, who have examined various parts of it. As noted, Boudet studied several of its treatises, as did Charles Burnett, Lauri Ockenström, Vajra Regan, Julien Véronèse, and others.[76] The manuscript's remarkable diversity of sources has drawn particular attention, and the fact that it appears to incorporate treatises known to have circulated together – that is, within close geographical proximity – has made it a compelling case study, often understood as preserving a textual tradition that stretches back at least two centuries. Indeed, some of its sections correspond to eleventh-century Hebrew and Aramaic texts, while others align with known earlier Arabic works.[77] In what follows, I wish to discuss another work that Pingree classified as Arabic, primarily based on its short prologue.

The treatise under discussion, which is untitled in the manuscript but which I will refer to as *The Book of Seven Names* (Liber septem nominum), or simply *The Seven Names*, following Thorndike's identification,[78] has received little scholarly attention and was only recently discussed in detail by Burnett in an article devoted to writing materials and processes in magical texts.[79] Unlike Pingree, who argued for a lost Arabic origin of the work, Burnett has proposed an ultimate Hebrew origin – an argument I wish to develop further through a close examination of the text itself, presented here with an edition and translation in the appendix of this Element.

---

[75] Thorndike, "Traditional Medieval Tracts."
[76] See, among others, Boudet, "Liber Bileth"; Burnett, "Inscriptio"; Ockenström and Regan, "The Hermetic Origins."
[77] For the Hebrew and Aramaic texts, see Sofer, *Solomonic Magic*, chapter 4. For the Arabic ones, see Ockenström and Regan, "The Hermetic Origins."
[78] A treatise of this name with the same attribution appears in the *Speculum Astronomiae*. See Thorndike, "Traditional Medieval Tracts," 253; Pingree, "Learned Magic," 46.
[79] Burnett, "Inscriptio." See also Weill-Parot, *Les "images astrologiques,"* 56.

The Seven Names is a short work attributed to a figure with an Arabic – and more specifically, Islamic – name: Muḥammad ibn al-Ḥasan ibn al-Ma'mūn (given in Latin as Muḥamet filius Alhascen et filius Amoemen, § 1).[80] The name appears within a long chain of transmission, a literary feature typical of Arabic literature. Such chains, attributing the work to a sequence of named authorities, are known in Islamic literature as *isnād*. A work that opens with such an extended list of names – all are clearly transliterations of common Arabic names – could almost automatically be classified as an "Arabic work," as Pingree indeed considered it.[81]

Mindful of the "Geber problem." – and of medieval compilers' habit of crediting their own work to renowned authorities[82] – we should approach apparent authorial attributions with caution. When a Latin treatise is called an "Arabic work," even though no Arabic exemplar survived, that label signals a hypothesis rather than a documented process of transmission. Because attributions were shaped by the compiler's historical and cultural setting, each case should be tested on three levels: (1) the manuscript's provenance, (2) the intellectual milieu that encouraged a given ascription, and (3) a close reading of the text itself. In the absence of an Arabic witness, I would prefer to use "multicultural magic" that signals the presence of several traditions without implying a homogeneous Arabic source that cannot be demonstrated at the present time.

The label "Arabic work" can be helpful as shorthand, yet – if left undefined – it may blur the very historical, cultural, and religious contexts we hope to illuminate. Does "Arabic" in a given case refer to a pre-Islamic setting, an Islamic milieu, a linguistic layer, or something else? In a Latin manuscript, the term cannot describe the script itself; it signals a presumed Arabic-language source. Unless we also specify where, when, by whom, and for whom that putative source was produced, the label remains hypothetical rather than evidentiary. In the case of *The Seven Names*, I suggest that a close reading of the text may reveal a complex history of transmission A careful examination – particularly one that considers the introduction as an integral part of the text itself, rather than treating it as a piece of metadata or a historical record – allows us to reflect on the possible historical and geographical context in which this work was composed. Yet, inevitably, this hypothesis must remain a hypothesis until further evidence comes to light, as research continues to progress.

---

[80] All references to sections refer to the annotated edition in Appendix A.
[81] Pingree, "Learned Magic," 46.
[82] Or, using Burnett's words (Burnett, "Arabic Magic," 82): "The authors of texts on magic tended to hide under the names of ancient sages (Hermes, Apollonius, Enoch, etc.), and the translators of the texts were also wary about revealing their identities."

Before turning to the text itself, it is worth pausing to consider the function of prologues and attributions within this codex, where such features appear. The Florentine manuscript comprises approximately forty-nine treatises and experiments, some of which are explicitly attributed to specific figures, while others are not. Generally speaking, short recipes and experiments tend to lack such attributions, while longer treatises are more likely to include them.[83] For example, the *Liber de locutione cum spiritibus planetarum* (Book on Conversation with the Spirits of the Planets) is presented as the sayings of "Abuelabec Altanarani, a certain philosopher and astrologer, [who] spoke about what he found in the books of the ancients."[84] Pingree discussed this attribution to Abuelabec Altanarani, whom he identified as al-Ṭabarānī, noting that this figure is also cited in the Picatrix. Although in that context the material is incorporated alongside other sources, it is still attributed to al-Ṭabarānī.[85]

Other treatises in the Florentine Codex are attributed to more "distant" figures – some biblical, others divine. Consider, for example, the *Liber de secretis angelorum* (The Book on the Secrets of the Angels), which is said to have been given to Adam by the angel Rachael (that is, Raziel).[86] Such an attribution plays a role in the history of the text, as well as its cultural context.[87] Another example is a treatise often classified as "Solomonic," but is in fact attributed to the disciples of Solomon: "Here begins the treatise of the disciples of Solomon, that is, Fortunatus, Eleazarus, Macarus, and Toz Grecus."[88] It seems evident here that the author – possibly inspiring Berengar Ganell, who was familiar with this work – sought to signal the different sources upon which he drew: Latin (Fortunatus, Macarus), Hebrew (Eleazar), and Greek (Toz). In another version of this treatise, preserving the same attribution, we indeed find ritual formulas composed of Hebrew liturgical phrases alongside Greek *nomina magica*.[89] As we have already seen, authors were aware of the nature of their sources, and attributions were often employed to frame a work in a particular way.

---

[83] For a useful review of the codex, see Véronèse, *L'Almandal*, 69–73.

[84] Florence, Biblioteca Nazionale Centrale, II.III.214 (henceforth: BNC, 31r: "Dixit Abuelabec Altanarani, quidam philosophus astrologus que, de hoc quod invenit in libris antiquorum." Also quoted by Véronèse, *L'Almandal*, 71.

[85] See Pingree, "Al-Ṭabarī," 106.

[86] It is, of course, a part of *Liber Razielis*. See Pingree, "Learned Magic," 47–48.

[87] See, for example, the discussion in Page, "Uplifting Souls," 86–89; Boudet and Véronèse, "Le secret dans la magie rituelle médiévale."

[88] BNC, 26v: "Incipit tractatus discipulorum Salomonis scilicet Fortunati, Eleazari, Macari et Toç Greci."

[89] On this work, see Boudet, *Entre science et nigromance*, 145–149; Véronèse, "La transmission," 201–202; Sofer, "*Ydea Salomonis*."

In the case of Ganell, this is reflected in the Saracen recipe he invented; in the case of the *Ydea Salomonis*, it is reflected in the author's prologue and deliberate incorporation of different traditions – Latin, Hebrew, and Greek – to construct a ritual.

This is not the only instance in which the Florentine Codex reflects this somewhat "inclusive" approach by hinting at or mentioning foreign sources. Another treatise, the *Liber Bileth* (The Book of Bileth), which instructs practitioners on how to summon the demonic king Bileth, contains an interesting formula that may offer insight into the author's identity and cultural background – or at least into his proficiency in different languages: "And for this reason we sit in this circle, and so that you may reveal to us everything present, past, and future – in Hebrew, Greek, and Latin – with the most perfect and wholly intelligible knowledge."[90] Here, the author seems to associate himself, and perhaps those with whom he shared this knowledge, with individuals capable of communicating in one or more of these languages. Of course, this gesture of inclusion is simultaneously an act of exclusion: We might wonder why Arabic is absent from a text that elsewhere refers to figures well-known from Arabic literature, such as Hārūt and Mārūt.[91] In any case, the awareness of foreign languages (as both relevant to the practitioner and as markers of written traditions) left clear traces in the text. This often contributed to the creation of genesis narratives, or to the attribution of a text to particular figures, shaping the work's structure and reception.

Having considered some of the prologues and attributions found in various treatises within this codex, let us now turn to *The Seven Names* and its content. The treatise sets out a relatively straightforward theory: God assigned one of His seven names to each day of the week, making each day distinct and uniquely suited to specific forms of magical practice. In other words, ritual activity performed on a particular day – by invoking its corresponding divine name – will produce a specific, well-defined result. This is presented as grounded in the cosmic structure organized around the number seven: God created seven seas, seven heavens, and seven earths. He also created seven spheres, or circles (*VII circuli*), each governed by a specific angel. By that, the introduction argues for a connection between the seven names of God and this cosmic system of seven, which "all time runs through" (§ 1). Properly using each name requires specific ritual

---

[90] BNC, 82v: "Et propter hoc in isto circula sedimus, et ad sciendum omne presens, preteritum et futurum, hebrayce, grece et latyne cum perfectissima et in omni intelligibili sciante." See also Boudet, "Liber Bileth," 340.
[91] See Boudet, "Liber Bileth," 326–327; Sofer, *Solomonic Magic*, chapter 8.

actions (writing on specific materials, fasting, bathing, suffumigation, and exorcism) to harness its power. Aligned with the sacred order of the days, triplicities, angels, winds, and stars, these rituals aim to invoke miracles, from healing and protection to love, war, and other concerns.

Following the brief prologue, the treatise proceeds systematically: Each of the seven names is discussed in relation to the specific day on which it must be used, beginning with the Sabbath (Saturday). Sometimes, the cosmological framework introduced in the prologue is recalled. For example, the second name is to be used on Sunday, and the text notes that it "is placed in the sixth heaven, and its angel is in the sixth heaven, who, with this name, adores the Creator" (§ 3). This return to the cosmological structure outlined in the introduction, however, gradually disappears. In the case of the fourth, fifth, and sixth names, there is no further mention of their placement within the heavens.

This cosmological framing returns only with the seventh and final name, which is said to be established in the highest heaven. On the surface, this structure might suggest a gradual ascent or hierarchy of names, increasing in power. Yet the organization of the treatise does not consistently support this reading. It even appears to contradict it, since the first name is described as the greatest of all (§ 2), without any reference to its location within the cosmic order.

In each of the initial sections on the seven names (§§ 2–8), the names themselves are conspicuously absent. Instead, the text instructs practitioners on their ritual use, typically to write them on surfaces like parchment or clay with natural materials, some of which appear in Latinized Arabic forms, as Burnett has noted.[92] In some cases, the names also require specific suffumigation. For example, the seventh name, associated with Venus, must be written on sheep parchment using ink made of egg, and suffumigated with aloe and sandalwood (§ 8). These kinds of instructions are typical of magical recipes circulating in the period. What sets *The Seven Names* apart, however, and distinguishes it from other recipe collections, is the overarching narrative and theoretical framework concerning the divine names.

As a practical manual, this treatise is certainly not a beginner's guide. While some instructions are given in considerable detail, the intended purpose of each operation is not always explicitly stated, and is sometimes only implied. For instance, a recipe is described as merely "pertaining to the name of the Sabbath day" (§ 2). For a student of astrology, this would

---

[92] Burnett, "Inscriptio."

not be difficult to infer; Saturday is governed by Saturn, and thus familiarity with the Saturnian qualities would enable the practitioner to discern which operations were appropriate for that day. This principle is made explicit in some instances. For example, the seventh name, associated with Friday, is connected to the qualities of Venus: "But this name is especially granted to womanly love" (§ 8). Yet the application of this logic is far from consistent: Other names are also linked to "womanly love" (§ 5, § 12).

It is precisely this overarching theory and its characteristic "bundling" of practices that call for careful examination. A close reading of the text reveals that the treatise – a compilation of scattered recipes – bears traces of editorial intervention. The inconsistencies throughout the work are often striking and sometimes confusing, suggesting that we are dealing with a text that has been edited, reworked, and possibly left incomplete. This would also help explain the most conspicuous absence: The seven names themselves – the very foundation of the treatise – are never actually provided within the text.[93]

The inconsistencies within the treatise become most apparent when we compare its first part (§§ 2–8), which describes the seven names and their ritual use, with its second part (§§ 9–15) and third part (§§ 16–30). The second part focuses primarily on the exorcisms that must accompany the use of each of the seven names. Structurally, it corresponds to the first part: Each of the seven paragraphs provides the exorcism associated with the respective name introduced earlier. However, this part also introduces entirely new elements – sometimes contradictory to what has been previously described – that were not mentioned in the first part. For instance, the practitioner is now instructed to inscribe a set of "rings" as part of the writing process (§ 9). In several cases, these additions contrast with the material introduced in the first section, raising further questions about the treatise's coherence and transmission history. Let us examine such a case more closely.

According to the first part of the treatise, the third name, which corresponds to the moon, "presides over those crossing roads and those who become lost in the sea, or crossing it, and merchants" (§ 4). The figures listed here share a common theme – movement and travel. While this passage does not explicitly state when the name should be written, it is implied (in line with the treatise's general structure) that it should be

---

[93] One possibility, raised by the anonymous reviewer, is that the compiler deliberately omitted the names to preserve them for oral transmission. In our case, however, that explanation seems less persuasive: *The Seven Names* includes many other formulas in full.

inscribed on the corresponding day, that is, Monday. Such instructions are either explicitly stated (§ 3, § 6, § 7) or implied (§ 2) for most of the names in the first part.

However, the second part of the treatise, which discusses the exorcism associated with the third name, introduces entirely different purposes. Here, the third name is said to be effective in addressing kings or for use in war. Most strikingly, the exorcism itself functions as a love spell: "That the heart of that N., daughter of that N., may serve me" (§ 11). Moreover, the text states that the third name may also be written on the day of Venus (Friday) to be used for love magic – a clear departure from the cosmological framework laid out in the first part.

This inconsistency is not limited to the third name. The treatment of the fourth name offers another striking example of the contradiction between the two parts of the work. In the first part, the reader is instructed to write this name – associated with Mars – using the blood of a dove (§ 5). Yet, in the second part, the practitioner is told to write it with saffron, musk, and aloe (§ 12). Such inconsistencies are scattered throughout the treatise, with some of the most significant differences appearing between its first and second parts.

The third part of the treatise continues along the lines of these phenomena, further complicating the structure and coherence of the work. It begins with general preparatory requirements expected of any practitioner of this art (*magisterio*), which include bathing, fasting, and suffumigating (§ 16). Similar instructions already appeared in the first part of the treatise, but they are not always consistent. For instance, while the third part instructs practitioners to fast and bathe for three days before any operation, the second part prescribes, in the case of the fifth name, only a single day of preparation (§ 13).

The third part of *The Seven Names* goes beyond general instructions, offering name-specific rites (§§ 17–22). Its content raises questions about whether it was part of the treatise's original design. It introduces a different theoretical framework, one that is briefly echoed in the second part, centered on the triplicities (the year's four seasons, each with three months). Unlike the first part, which is structured around the number seven, this section emphasizes the seasons as the cosmic forces behind the recipes and their efficacy.

Perhaps the most striking indication that this third part may represent a text of separate origin is the explicit reference to another book: "And this is the book of Heh'eben, son of Joseph, the greatest sage, and through this divine knowledge he knew the days and wet years" (§ 16). Here, the author explicitly attributes the theory of triplicities and the associated knowledge to an otherwise unidentified sage, Heh'eben son of Joseph (Yaḥyā ibn Yūsuf?) – a figure that is entirely absent from the earlier parts of the treatise.

The striking inconsistencies found throughout the treatise – on practical, theoretical, and structural levels – strongly suggest that we are dealing with distinct traditions that were brought together. Unlike the first part, the second and third parts of the treatise appear to share more in common, particularly in their use of the theory of triplicities. Before turning to this aspect, however, I would like to highlight some of the explicit Arabic references within the text.

Beyond the Arabic *isnād* found in the prologue, *The Seven Names* mentions other well-known Arabic figures. In the second part, specifically in the paragraph concerning the first name (§ 9), there is a clear allusion to the Abbasid caliph Hārūn ar-Rashīd, here referred to as "King Aron [or Haaron] in the East." The same passage states that a philosopher and astrologer named Algorismus (the common Latin form of the name of the renowned mathematician Al-Khwārizmī)[94] attributed the first name to one of Hārūn's prisoners. While Al-Khwārizmī is known to have worked in the Abbasid House of Wisdom, this activity took place after Hārūn's death.[95] It remains unclear whether this passage draws on any existing tradition in either Latin or Arabic sources, but its central logic relies on two notions: Al-Khwārizmī's reputation as a scholar and the prisoner's power to overcome or influence the king who imprisoned him. Interestingly, this theme does not align consistently within the treatise itself: According to the first part (§ 7), the sixth name is associated with influencing kings, while in the second part (§ 11), it is the third name that is linked to this power. This again underscores the internal inconsistencies between the different sections of the work.

As previously noted, several of the ingredients mentioned in *The Seven Names* appear in Latin transliteration from Arabic, with varying degrees of clarity and accuracy. For instance, the reference to parchment made of *areignum* likely derives from *al-ǧanam* ("sheep"), while the day *Alcoara* seems to stem from *az-zuhara* ("Venus"). This pattern is not limited to *termini technici* or *materia magica*, but also extends to certain verbal formulas. For example, the exorcism of the fourth name (§ 12) opens with unmistakably Arabic words: "Bisam Yley Eulum Escelectum" – the

---

[94] Burnett, "John of Seville and John of Spain," 64 n. 25.
[95] On Al-Khwārizmī, see Berggren, "Mathematics and Her Sisters," 403–413.

first words being a transliteration of the well-known Islamic formula *bi-smi 'llāh* ("in the name of Allah"). Moreover, some of the angelic names that appear in the text also seem to reflect Arabic forms. One notable case is "Scellim L'eli Acimaleycum," where the author presents them as names of angels. Yet their linguistic form suggests otherwise, particularly the *-aleycum* ending in the third name, which echoes the Arabic *'alaykum* ("upon you"). This may point to a greeting formula, with *Scellim* deriving from *as-salāmu* ("peace"), a not uncommon formula in rituals involving encounters with angelic or demonic figures.[96]

The exorcism of the sixth name (§ 14) further supports this observation, as it contains a formula that again draws directly on Arabic. The phrase "Bis Mellah" is another transliteration of *bi-smi 'llāh*, followed by the invocation of angels whose names correspond to *Mīkā'īl* (Uuremich'l) and *'Isrāfīl* (Uuescerafil). This Arabic resonance is reinforced not only by the names of the angels but also by the description of their appearance in the same passage: "Their heads are in the heavens, and their feet touch the ends and boundaries of the earth, and their wings touch the East and the West." Such imagery is well attested in Islamic tradition. Consider, for example, Abū Manṣūr al-Daylamī's *Musnad al-Firdaws*, a collection of hadiths, where one finds a similar description of an angelic figure (the "cockerel"): "Its feet are on the boundaries of the lowest [earth] and its folded neck is under the Throne; its wings are in the East and the West."[97]

What can we learn from this intercultural encounter, in which a Latin-writing author, most likely Christian, incorporates Islamic formulas? Is it merely an isolated case? Moreover, is there evidence to determine whether this interaction is direct or indirect? The presence of Arabic terms and formulas strongly suggests that an Arabic treatise may have been translated here, possibly inspiring Pingree's view that *The Seven Names* originated in Arabic. Yet, as I have argued, such an assumption may overshadow other clues indicating a more complex process of cultural exchange that shaped *The Seven Names*. One might wonder why, if the author was a skilled translator, certain formulaic passages fail so noticeably. Copying errors could explain some instances, such as the transformation of *bi-smi llāh* into "Bisam Yley," but that rationale falters when we consider examples like "Scellim L'eli Acimaleycum," which the author interpreted as angels. Indeed, at least some aspects of *The Seven Names* – already identified as comprising two or perhaps three different parts – complicate the notion of

---

[96] Cf. the Latin formula "pax vobis" that appears in *Liber Bileth* in the Florentine Codex. See Boudet, "Liber Bileth," 332 and 343.
[97] Burge, *Angels in Islam*, 189.

a straightforward, complete translation from Arabic into Latin. Further evidence of intercultural exchange, this time likely reflecting Jewish traditions, challenges the notion of a straightforward translation and invites a more nuanced reading of *The Seven Names*. These traces not only complicate the idea of a wholly Arabic (Islamic) source but also offer clues about the cultural environment, and perhaps even the time and place, in which this work took shape.

I would like to highlight three instances in *The Seven Names* that demonstrate an engagement with Jewish textual traditions. The first concerns the first name that is associated with the Sabbath, which is described here as the day on which Moses received the Torah (§ 2). In the Babylonian Talmud, Rava (a Babylonian amora) asserts that "everyone agrees that the Torah was given to the Jewish people on Shabbat."[98] This notion recurs in Jewish sources from the Middle Ages onward, while both Muslims and Christians generally refuted the sanctity of Saturday as the holiest day of the week.[99]

Naturally, proposing to perform a ritual (particularly one involving writing and suffumigation) on the Sabbath would raise *halakhic* concerns for Jewish practitioners. Yet, as is well-known, such internal debates did not always prevent the practice of magic, and the question of which actions were permissible remained open to interpretation.[100] Still, as Ortal-Paz Saar has shown, Jewish authors often took care to avoid prescribing actions that would explicitly desecrate the Sabbath.[101] I suggest that *The Seven Names* reflects a similar sensitivity. A close reading of the treatise, especially when considering its three parts together, indicates that – unlike the other days – there is no explicit instruction to perform any ritual act on the day of Saturn (Saturday). While the first part does not consistently specify that the name associated with each day must be written precisely on that day (e.g., Sunday in § 3, Wednesday in § 6), the third part adopts a more uniform and structured pattern – and omits Saturday altogether. This final part lists the days of the week alongside their associated powers but excludes any instructions for Saturday, suggesting a deliberate avoidance that aligns with Jewish concerns over Sabbath observance.

The second case that shows signs of an engagement with Jewish textual traditions appears in the second part of the treatise, which contains various exorcisms and verbal formulas to be used. As we have

---

[98] Babylonian Talmud, Sabbath 86b.
[99] The notion of a sacred weekday was often raised in Jewish-Christian-Islamic polemical writings. See, among others, Goldziher, "The Sabbath Institution in Islam."
[100] Bohak, *Ancient Jewish Magic*, 370–372; Harari, *Jewish Magic*, 356–358, 391–392, and 416.
[101] Saar, *Love Magic*, 246–247.

already seen, some of these formulas are undoubtedly Arabic, and there is at least one easily recognizable Greek word – Ἅγιον (§ 10). Another formula, found in the exorcism of the third name (§ 11), is composed of both Hebrew and Aramaic passages, drawing primarily on biblical texts, though not exclusively. The author's transliteration practices complicate identification: Words are frequently merged or split, and vowels are commonly doubled, yet there is a certain consistency in the representation of specific Hebrew letters. For example, "uu" for ו, "sc," "sh," or "ss" for ש, and "x," "xc," or "xh" for ח/כ.[102] Because of this instability (the splitting or merging of words), identifying the Hebrew or Aramaic phrases can be difficult. Nonetheless, the formula (Ane Adonay formula) begins with what is clearly a prayer, though only partially recognizable at first glance:

The formula: Ane Adonay Jelohim Jeloy Ebraym and Ysaach and Israel Uueiloy Moyse Uuaharon Uueyloy …

Hebrew (transliterated): Ane Adonay 'elohim 'elohei 'avraham veyitzḥaq veyisra'el ve'elohei moshe ve'aharon ve'elohei …

Translation: Answer, O Lord God, God of Abraham, Isaac, and Israel, and God of Moses and Aaron, and God of …

After this passage, not found in biblical sources but in liturgical and magical ones, *The Seven Names* continues with biblical verses (Adonay Bamar formula). The first one is Numbers 12:6–8:

The formula: Adonay Bamar Esloy Ydi Ydda Jeahalum and Deburbulohhun Abda Moyse Uahhol Batunamehun Uuefalel Faed Debir Uuebrai Uuelubabi Duth Uuetham Unet Adonay Iabieth

Hebrew (transliterated): Adonay bamar'a 'elav 'etvada' baḥalom 'adaber bo. Lo khen 'avdi moshe bekhol beiti ne'eman hu. Pe 'el pe 'adaber bo umar'e velo veḥidot utemunat Adonay yabbit

Translation (NIV): I, the Lord, reveal myself to them in visions, I speak to them in dreams. But this is not true of my servant Moses; he is faithful in all my house. With him I speak face-to-face, clearly and not in riddles; he sees the form of the Lord.

In this case, we can observe how the author interpreted the letters "et" as the conjunction "and" rather than as part of a single word "[et]Debur[ ]bu" (that is, 'adaber bo),[103] reflecting both an oral transmission of the text

---

[102] Interestingly, there is inconsistency with "and" – sometimes translated into Latin ("et"), but sometimes left as the prefix "uu" (as in Hebrew).

[103] It is evident that the author interpreted it as such, as he utilized his standard symbol for "et" instead of writing out the letters.

and a splitting of what was originally a single word (*adabber* → *atdaber* → *et daber*), further merged with the next three words ("bulohhun," that is, "bo Lo khen"). Following four words I was unable to identify at first (Uehuuegale Imilxate formula), the author cites the Aramaic of Daniel 2:22, and immediately afterward, Daniel 2:21:

The formula: Uehuuegale Imilxate Uemes Cetrethe Iedha Mebahsol'ia Udenaora Amisere. Uueh'scy Mehehtuete and Danie Uuethdimine Methe Adde Maichxcein Uueema Hal'um Mallxhim Ieib K'hohmethe Lethalxmin Uuemandaya Lyeydaa Bieteuuete

Aramaic (transliterated): Hu gale 'amiqata umesatterata yada' ma vahashokha unehora 'imeh shere. Vehu mehashne 'idanaya vezimnaya meha'de malkhin umehaqeim malkhin yahev hakhemeta lehakimin umande'a leyade'ei bina

Translation (NIV): He reveals deep and hidden things; he knows what lies in darkness, and light dwells with him. He changes times and seasons; he deposes kings and raises up others. He gives wisdom to the wise and knowledge to the discerning.

The verses from Daniel seem to resonate with the aim mentioned in the same paragraph. According to this paragraph, the name can benefit those who address the king.[104] These biblical verses are commonly cited in recipes for dream requests.[105]

These formulas raise the question of whether we are indeed dealing with a Hebrew, Aramaic, or Arabic recipe for dream requests, even though *The Seven Names* itself does not specify this purpose. The intersection of these three languages frequently appears in the Cairo Genizah, a vast collection of texts preserved in the attic of the Ben Ezra Synagogue in Fustat, Old Cairo.[106] While searching for a possible parallel in the Genizah, I came across a twelfth-century fragment – an amulet or spell for dream requests – written in Judeo-Arabic, yet quoting Hebrew and Aramaic biblical verses.[107] In light of this parallel, we can identify some of the Latin phrases. For instance, "Symenac Daniari Amacye Beuyaium" corresponds

---

[104] Salzer, *Die Magie der Anspielung*, 133–134.
[105] Bellusci, "Jewish Oneiric Divination," 123–124.
[106] On the magical texts in this Genizah, see Bohak, "Towards a Catalogue"; Peter Schäfer and Shaul Shaked's three-volume *Magische Texte aus der Kairoer Geniza*. In the context of Arabic and Judeo-Arabic texts that were also available in Latin translations, see the introduction of Bohak and Burnett, *Thābit ibn Qurra*.
[107] Cambridge Library, T-S AS 143.225. The fragment was published and studied by Shaked, "On Jewish Literature of Magic in Muslim Countries"; Bellusci, "Jewish Oneiric Divination," 123–124; Bellusci, "Dream Requests," 64–69.

to the Hebrew *shim'u na devarai 'im yihye nevi'akhem*, the beginning of Numbers 12:7, which is almost unrecognizable in the Latin transliteration. Still, the texts are not entirely alike: In the fragment, the order of the verses from Daniel is not reversed, as it is in *The Seven Names*. Moreover, some of the Judeo-Arabic passages in the Latin text are transliterations, whereas others are translations (see later in this section).[108] In any case, this would not be the first time that materials currently known exclusively (or almost exclusively) from the Cairo Genizah are attested in our Florentine Codex.[109]

One might argue that the Genizah fragment represents an earlier form of *The Seven Names*. Yet this fragment includes a self-contained passage, lacking evidence that it belongs to a larger treatise like *The Seven Names*. Alternatively, it could reflect the work of a practitioner following instructions from an earlier version of the treatise. If so, the magician did not strictly follow those instructions, using paper instead of gazelle parchment and black ink instead of saffron-based ink. In either case, this parallel supports the earlier observation: The inconsistencies in *The Seven Names* reflect its composite nature, shaped by multiple recipes circulating in the same period and region.[110]

The third indication of an encounter with Jewish texts concerns primarily the third part of the work, which, as discussed, presents a different cosmological theory. This theory of triplicities (not unrelated to the astrological notion of triplicities) holds that "the blessed God called the first season spring, the second summer, the third autumn, the fourth winter, and assigned three months to each, [and] to each triplicity [he assigned] an angel, and to each angel three other assisting angels, and to each month an angel, who, in his month, serves his Lord" (§ 23). The treatise continues by listing these angels along with the names of the sun, moon, and the winds for each season.

Scholars of Arabic magic, especially those familiar with the so-called *corpus Bunianum* (works attributed to the famous Sufi Aḥmad al-Būnī), will recognize this theory from one of the most renowned treatises, the *Shams al-Maʿārif al-Kubrā,* which was probably compiled during the sixteenth century.[111] In its eighth chapter, the *Shams* emphasizes

---

[108] A more systematic comparison between the two is beyond the scope of this discussion.
[109] See Section 3.
[110] Interestingly, we find another treatise in the Genizah in which the number seven is used as an organizing principle of a set of recipes. I refer here to the *Seven Grades* (שבע המעלות), which is composed of Aramaic and Hebrew texts. See Bohak, "Babylonian Jewish Magic," 89.
[111] On the *corpus Bunianum*, see Gardiner, "Esotericism," 1–77; Coulon, *La magie en terre d'islam au Moyen Âge*, 205–232; Porter, Saif, and Savage-Smith, "Medieval Islamic

the importance of knowing how the year is divided into four triplicities (*ṭāqūfa*) and the names of the angels, winds, and celestial bodies – the sun and moon – that preside over each season.[112] Even the fixed duration of the seasons matches that found in the *Shams*, presented in a way that allows practitioners to determine the ideal time for their operations without requiring astronomical skills or instruments (§ 24):[113]

> The first triplicity is from the 24th of March until the 24th of June. The second is from that day until the 24th of September. The third is from that day until the 24th of December. The fourth is from that day until the 24th of March.

It appears that this text sets the boundaries of each season around the equinoxes and solstices, in line with a widespread medieval Christian custom. More specifically, it follows the Julian calendar's convention of fixing the turning points of the seasons on March 25, June 24, September 24, and December 25.[114] While it is tempting to argue for the presence of earlier Arabic materials that later found their way into the *Shams*, we must also consider another possibility, especially given the scholarly consensus that an unidentified Jewish source inspired this section of the *Shams*.

This influence is also reflected in the very term used in the *Shams* for these triplicities – *ṭāqūfa*, a loanword from the Hebrew *tequfa*, commonly used to designate the seasons (*tequfot* in the plural).[115] While Coulon rightly noted that *Sefer Razi'el HaMal'akh* (The Book of the Angel Raziel) could not have been the direct source for the *Shams*, as Georges Vajda suggested – given that it is a Hebrew composition from the sixteenth century – this does not rule out the possibility that an earlier tradition, also preserved in *Sefer Razi'el HaMal'akh*, influenced the *Shams*. I refer here to the Hebrew *Sefer HaTequfot*, which was translated into Latin in the thirteenth century and incorporated as the fourth book of *Liber Razielis*, under the title *Liber temporum* (The Book of the Seasons).[116]

The theory of triplicities is central to *Liber Razielis*, which instructs the practitioner concerning *The Book of the Seasons*: "And look in this book and study purely in it and you will obtain with the help of God all that

---

Amulets, Talismans, and Magic," 529–532. On the dating of the *Shams*, see also Gardiner, "Forbidden Knowledge," 123–129
[112] I have used the partial edition of Coullaut Cordero, "El Kitāb Šams al-Ma'ārif al-Kubrà."
[113] On this phenomenon, see Sofer, "Upon the Magician's Escritoire."
[114] McCluskey, *Astronomies and Cultures*, 24.
[115] Vajda, "Sur quelques éléments juifs et pseudo-juifs." See also the discussion by Coulon, "La magie islamique," 494–495, and Coulon, "Intégration et réception d'éléments juifs."
[116] On *Sefer HaTequfot* and its translation into Latin, see Sofer, "The Great Name."

you ask for."[117] The practitioners are urged to keep the book pure, and by doing so, they will not only gain many good things (*multa bona*), but also "inherit the life of the next world."[118] *The Book of the Seasons* then lists the names of the angels governing each season (cf. § 25), the names of the four winds in each season (cf. § 26), and the names of the sun and the moon in each season (cf. §§ 27–28), alongside other cosmological elements (e.g., the names of the sea and the earth).

A comparison between *The Seven Names* and *The Book of the Seasons* reveals that while there is little direct correspondence in the specific names – with only a few cases of partial overlap[119] – the broader cosmological framework is strikingly similar. Despite these differences in detail, the overarching structure of the triplicities, their associated cosmological features, and the way this theory is operationalized in practice suggest a shared conceptual basis underlying both works. If Vajda and Coulon are correct in their assessment, the third part of *The Seven Names* points to a Latin version of the theory of triplicities that predates the known Arabic materials on *tāqūfa* – potentially linked to *Liber Razielis*, a text that our author (or his source) seems to have known at least in part, given the citations preserved in the Florentine Codex.[120] These citations, which focus on the angels governing each month, circulated with *Sefer HaTequfot* in the thirteenth century, and were also incorporated into the Alfonsine *Liber Razielis* as part of *The Book of the Seasons*.[121]

The part in the Florentine Codex connected with *Liber Razielis* does not appear to derive directly from the Alfonsine version. It is therefore more plausible that the relevant passages in *The Seven Names* draw on material that was later adapted by the Alfonsine scribes – who might themselves, though this remains speculative, have contributed to the shaping or creation of *The Seven Names*. Another work in the same codex, likewise composed of at least two distinct texts and tied to materials found in the Cairo Genizah, appears to have undergone a comparable

---

[117] Vatican Reg. lat. 1300, 86r: "Et aspicias in isto libro et studeas munde in eo et obtinebis cum dei adiutorio omnia que petieris."
[118] Vatican Reg. lat. 1300, 85v: "Et cum omnibus aliis supradictis hereditabit vitam alterius seculi."
[119] Consider, for example, the names of the East. According to *The Seven Names*, in the first season it is Al'udum, while in *Liber Razielis* it appears as Atbedan (63v) or Abbadon (81r). In the fourth season, *The Seven Names* gives Mehhadi, whereas *Liber Razielis* lists Atritael (63v) or Madigac (81r).
[120] Under the title *Liber de secretis angelorum* (The Book on the Secrets of Angels) in BNC, 43v–44v. As Pingree has noted, Michael Scot was familiar with the text and its content. See Pingree, "Learned Magic," 47–48.
[121] Vatican Reg. lat. 1300, 49v–52v.

process of reworking within the Alfonsine scriptorium.[122] While these proposals remain tentative, they invite a reassessment of Pingree's classification of *The Seven Names* as belonging to the "new magic of Arabic origin."[123] Whether "Arabic" here refers narrowly to language or, more broadly, to a cultural context, *The Seven Names* resists any notion of a singular lineage or unambiguous origin.

Rather than a unified composition, *The Seven Names* is a compilation of varied materials – chiefly Jewish and Islamic – that seeks, yet ultimately fails, to integrate them into a coherent literary and theoretical framework. Its shortcomings are most evident in the marked inconsistencies and contradictions scattered throughout, as well as in the retention of two competing cosmological systems that might have been reconciled but were instead left side by side, leaving the potential practitioner with glaring gaps and confusion. At the same time, the very idea of dividing the material into seven parts – each seemingly linked to a different theme or practice – is not without precedent. It also appears in treatises preserved in the Cairo Genizah, such as *The Seven Grades*.[124] Yet here, in *The Seven Names*, we find a more ambitious attempt to weave these recipes together under a single, albeit loosely and inconsistently realized, guiding structure.

The Seven Names is not an Arabic text, but a Latin compilation that draws on various materials, reflecting encounters of different kinds among diverse cultures in distinct geographical regions. Although it incorporates (Judeo-)Arabic, Aramaic, and Hebrew formulas, it endeavors – much like Geber – to present itself as an Arabic work of supposedly lost Islamic origin, attributed to Muḥammad ibn al-Ḥasan. In addition to introducing an Islamic *isnād* in the prologue, it invokes eminent figures such as Al-Khwārizmī and Hārūn ar-Rashīd, thereby reinforcing its purported Arabic lineage, even if somewhat anachronistically. Moreover, the third part – chiefly on the theory of triplicities – is introduced (§ 16) as a tool for weather forecasting by the "greatest sage," whose name remains unidentified. This emphasis on astronomy reflects the scientific treatises of the time when such knowledge was greatly valued in agrarian societies.[125]

What looks like "ascription" was, for medieval compilers, a routine activation of the author function. As Foucault observed, the author's name works as "a certain functional principle by which, in our culture,

---

[122] I refer here to the two parts of *Liber Bileth*. See Sofer, *Solomonic Magic*, chapter 10.
[123] Pingree, "Learned Magic," 40.
[124] See above, n. 110.
[125] See Bos and Burnett, *Scientific Weather Forecasting in the Middle Ages*.

one limits, excludes, and chooses" among proliferating meanings.[126] By anchoring a composite treatise in the persona of Solomon, wise Saracens, Rabbi Akiva, or Muḥammad ibn al-Ḥasan, scribes were not forging authority but exercising this principle of selection, organizing fragments under a recognizable banner and thereby constraining the endless drift of signification that magical recipes invite. Much like Ganell, the author of *The Seven Names* positioned himself within the Arabic tradition he knew – directly or indirectly – by drawing on what he perceived as part of that tradition, without adhering to our modern standards of citation or faithful paraphrase. It remains unlikely, however, that our scribe copied his entire composition from a single Arabic text, and the translation process offers evidence for this; it often struggles to render certain terms (especially those referring to material substances), suggesting that the compiler was working from fragmented sources or oral and written traditions rather than translating a single Arabic original.

Additionally, certain details suggest that the author was reading from a text written in Hebrew script (of Hebrew or Judeo-Arabic texts). This is evident, for example, in the rendering of Miriam's name as "Myrus" (§ 11) – a form likely resulting from a misreading of the Hebrew final *mem* (ם) as *samekh* (ס). Such an exchange is unlikely to derive from misreading Arabic script. Furthermore, unlike the comparable spell preserved in the Cairo Genizah, *The Seven Names* presents a mixed approach to Judeo-Arabic passages: Some were translated into Latin, while others were merely transliterated. For instance, "And in the name most beloved to you" (ובאחב אסמאיך אליך) in the Genizah fragment was transliterated as "[Cyhce]byahbismay Cileihce," whereas "I mention you, God [of Israel], and your angels" (דכרתך יא רב [ישראל ו]מלאיכתך) was translated into Latin.[127]

Notably, while the Judeo-Arabic text explicitly refers to the night (fitting for a request to receive a revelation in a dream), *The Seven Names* remains more general. Where the former calls upon God's name to reveal "in this night what is in my mind" (הדא אלליה מא פי נפשי), the latter paraphrases the request, asking for "everything that I have in mind" (*de omni quod in mente habeo*, §11). These examples highlight a complex, multilayered translation process with aspects that remain obscure. One still unclear link – raised by the anonymous reviewer of this Element – is the possibility of an Arabic version standing between the Judeo-Arabic or Hebrew

---

[126] Foucault, "What Is an Author?" 221.
[127] See the edition in Appendix A, §11.

materials and the surviving Latin.[128] Whether such an intermediary once existed, describing *The Seven Names* simply as an "Arabic magic" text may not fully capture the complexity of its passage across languages and communities. With this background in mind, we may now turn to another riddle in the history of learned magic: the *Almandel*.

3 The *Almandel* Problem: Do We Have to Assume a Lost Source?

The Florentine Codex that preserves *The Seven Names* also contains other works, some of which are indeed translations of known Arabic texts. Notable examples are John of Seville's Latin translation of Thābit ibn Qurra's On *Talismans*,[129] and Pseudo-Plato's *The Book of the Cow*.[130] Both works circulated in Arabic, yet their Arabic recensions are themselves mosaics. Their presence in the codex confirms that complete Arabic-language treatises could reach Latin readers, without implying that this guarantees a single, homogeneous origin. Within that mixed environment, it is sensible to ask whether *The Seven Names* incorporates Arabic components. However, its evident blend of Hebrew, Judeo-Arabic, and Latin features cautions against positing a lone Arabic prototype. *The Seven Names* illustrates how compilation and translation can involve multiple stages of adaptation and borrowing, a complexity that the broad label "Arabic magic" can sometimes obscure. This is particularly true for works in which the state of evidence is poor, as is the case with another treatise preserved in the Florentine Codex: the *Almandel*.

Pingree, in his study of the Florentine Codex, identified the *Almandel* as one of the Arabic works translated into Latin during the thirteenth century, probably in Toledo.[131] The treatise instructs practitioners to construct an instrument called the *almandel* (or *almandal*), made from a square plate of red brass engraved with specific names. Holes are pierced in the plate to allow the smoke from the suffumigation beneath it to rise. An iron rod is placed upright at each corner, supporting a candle of a distinct color – green, red, saffron, and white – each inscribed with letters. A mixture of substances is burned under the *almandel*, which is suffumigated and

---

[128] Some details, however, complicate that scenario. For instance, the compiler reads the Arabic "Scellim L'eli Acimaleycum" as a set of angelic names, a move that seems less likely if he were working from an Arabic exemplar. Such features weaken, though do not rule out, the case for an Arabic intermediary.
[129] Bohak and Burnett, *Thābit ibn Qurra*.
[130] Saif, "The Cows and the Bees."
[131] Pingree, "Learned Magic," 48.

consecrated with four exorcisms for seven days and nights. During this ritual, the candles are lit, and spirits, specifically *algin* and *asarin*, are summoned and commanded. Once the rite is completed, the *almandel* is wrapped and stored for use in specific recipes detailed by the author.

The very term *al-mandel* is known from Arabic sources, as we will discuss later, and so is the word *al-ǧinn*, referring to the well-known djinn.[132] William of Auvergne was familiar with this work; he explicitly referred to the *almandel* as an instrument, describing it in a way that closely matches the version found in the Florentine Codex. Taken together, this evidence makes a compelling case that we may indeed be dealing with an Arabic work that has survived only in this Latin translation, likely produced before William's reference to it. However, as the example of *The Seven Names* has demonstrated, such evidence must be approached with caution. The incorporation of Arabic elements – whether technical terms, ritual structures, or spirit names – does not presuppose the existence of a single Arabic original. As we shall see, a close examination of the texts suggests another reasonable hypothesis.

Scholarly works on the *Almandel* did not end with Pingree's brief comments. In 2012, Julien Véronèse published a groundbreaking study on the *Almandel* of the Florentine Codex, arguing that it is composed of two (independent) parts: the *Liber in figura almandal et eius opere* (The Book concerning the Almandal and its Operation) and the *Alius liber de almandal* (Another Book of the Almandal).[133] According to Véronèse, these two parts may derive from two distinct Arabic sources that the translator combined, given their strong parallels and structural similarities. They are, however, clearly independent compositions, and the scribe himself seems aware of this, designating the second part as *alius* – that is, an alternative version.[134]

Despite the overall similarity between these two parts – essentially, two distinct versions – Véronèse highlighted several differences, especially in the construction of the *almandel* itself. For example, in the first version, the candles must be of different colors and inscribed with letters, whereas in the second version, this requirement is absent.[135] Véronèse labels these two versions collectively as "version F," a term we will adopt here.

Version F, or a closely related source, had a profound impact on later Christian practitioners, who extensively reworked and expanded the

---

[132] Véronèse, *L'Almandal*, 16–18.
[133] Ibid.; Veenstra, "The Holy Almandal."
[134] BNC, 77r. See also Véronèse, *L'Almandal*, 87.
[135] Véronèse, *L'Almandal*, 20–26.

text to create what Véronèse terms "version F2," preserved in a single manuscript.[136] As Véronèse shows, this reworked version integrates material from version F with contemporary Latin *nigromantic* texts, including the well-known *Ars Notoria*.[137] This version laid the foundation for an even more widespread form – sometimes titled *The Book of Intelligences* (Liber Intelligentiarum) or simply the *Almadel* – which survives in several manuscripts, not only in fifteenth-century Latin but also in later Hebrew and English translations (Figure 4).[138]

Through detailed textual analysis, Véronèse reconstructs three main phases of the Latin (Christian) adaptation of the *Almandel*, likely composed in the second half of the fourteenth century, probably in Northern Italy, and later disseminated across Italy and Germany.[139] Ultimately, this Christian tradition traces its conceptual origins to an Arabic prototype that was translated and subsequently lost. Yet, as Véronèse also observes, the version that arguably preserves this Arabic origin most directly – version F – shares relatively little with the later Christian adaptations. Moreover, all of these versions are attested only from the fifteenth century onward. This poor state of evidence is characteristic of many texts of "Solomonic magic," leaving us with a limited degree of certainty, a condition unlikely to change unless new sources are discovered.[140]

Years after Véronèse's study, a new and significant discovery was indeed made – not of the lost Arabic source, but, perhaps surprisingly, of a thirteenth-century Latin-Christian version of the *Almandel*. In 2018, Vajra Regan identified a thirteenth-century manuscript containing what he argued to be an early Christian adaptation of the *Almandel*.[141] This version, preserved within a larger lapidary treatise (*De coloribus et virtutibus lapidum*), instructs practitioners in the preparation of a portable altar designed to restore lost or weakened virtues to stones. While this text does not use the term *almandel* but rather *areola*, its description of the altar closely parallels the instrument described in version F and in the later versions of the *Almandel* tradition. This is, to date, the earliest surviving manuscript that appears to describe a ritual practice involving such a portable altar, with several distinctive details already in place.

---

[136] Florence, Biblioteca Medicea Laurenziana, Plut. 89, sup. 38, 268r–278v.
[137] Véronèse, *L'Almandal*, 30–34.
[138] Ibid., 34–48; Veenstra, "The Holy Almandal." For the Hebrew texts, see Sofer, "The Hebrew Manuscripts," 138–140.
[139] Véronèse, *L'Almandal*, 37–40.
[140] Véronèse, "La transmission."
[141] Regan, "The De consecratione lapidum."

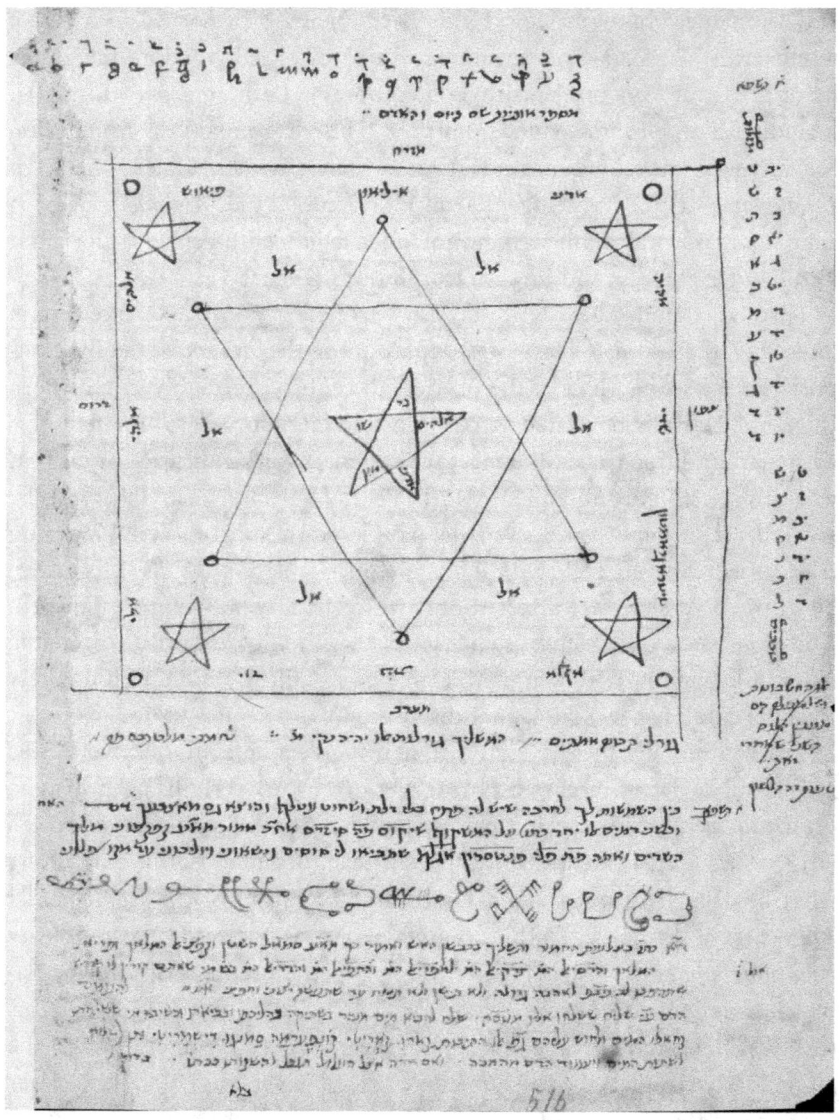

Figure 4 A Hebrew *Almadel* (Geneva, Bibliothèque de Genève, Comites Latentes 145).

In addition, Damaris Gehr has published an interesting study challenging Véronèse's reconstruction. Gehr argues that the *Almandel* was originally a lost Hebrew work, which was later adapted with Arabic material.[142] More specifically, she argued that Berengar Ganell was aware of

---

[142] Gehr, "Gaudent brevitatem moderni."

an *Almandel* tradition circulating in thirteenth-century Spain, which had been translated from Hebrew into Latin. Based on this argument, Gehr concludes that the most widespread textual tradition of the *Almandel* – namely, the *Liber Intelligentiarum* – can ultimately be traced back to this hypothesized Jewish origin.

The ongoing scholarly debate over the *Almandel*, with its mixture of concrete textual evidence and speculative reconstruction, reflects the challenges posed by the fragmentary state of the sources and the assumptions made in the course of their interpretation. In light of this complex landscape, and in an effort to reconsider some of these assumptions, I will begin by revisiting Gehr's argument before proposing an alternative narrative for the history of the *Almandel*.

Gehr's argument is quite knotty and rests on several assumptions, some of which are not fully articulated. As noted, she proposes the existence of a lost Hebrew work that preceded the Latin translation of the *Almandel* in the thirteenth century. According to Gehr, Jewish practitioners were familiar with, and actively engaged in, a ritual practice similar to the *Almandel*. This claim is primarily based on a sixteenth-century manuscript containing excerpts from Ganell's *Summa*, in which the *Almandel* is referred to in three languages – Arabic (*almandel*), Hebrew (*alemelagyn*), and Latin (*ara consecracionum*). Gehr argues that the presence of a Hebrew term for the *Almandel* indicates Jewish knowledge of either the instrument itself or a text concerning it. She further suggests that the Hebrew term *alemelagyn* may represent a hybrid formation, combining the Arabic *almandel* with the Hebrew *malakhim* (angels), reflecting a Jewish adaptation of the term.

Moreover, since this passage in Ganell's *Summa* is attributed to *verba Salomonis* ("the sayings of Solomon"), Gehr contends that this lends further weight to her argument. It implies that the term *alemelagyn* predates Ganell, who merely transmitted this older tradition, thereby indicating an earlier Hebrew familiarity with the concept. To support her case, Gehr also draws parallels between the cosmological framework of *Sefer HaRazim* (late antiquity) and the *Almandel*, particularly their shared association of Mercury with twelve celestial altitudes inhabited by angels. While she acknowledges the complexities introduced by pseudepigraphy, she nonetheless points to certain scribal practices that mark a specifically Jewish phase in the transmission of the text (e.g., authors arguing for a Hebrew origin).

There are several reasons to reconsider Gehr's proposal. First, the reliability of the sixteenth-century manuscript of the *Summa* she cites must be questioned, as the earliest known manuscript does not include the excerpts in question due to loss of folios. This later version, therefore, appears to reflect a speculative reconstruction of a presumed lost passage. Even if one accepts this reconstruction, the presence of a Hebrew term for the *Almandel*, the *alemelagyn*, should be approached with more caution. The author of the manuscript appears to be intent on establishing multilingual correspondences, and the term itself does not convincingly derive from Hebrew. Moreover, Jewish familiarity with the *Almandel* (in the form of *Liber Intelligentiarum*), using the Hebrew transliteration אלמנדל (*almandel*), is already attested in the fifteenth century. This undermines the necessity of positing *alemelagyn* as evidence for a distinct or earlier Jewish version.

The claim that *verba Salomonis* refers to a concrete source behind Ganell's text is also problematic. The existence of such a source is, at best, uncertain.[143] More critically, Gehr's cosmological comparison between *Sefer HaRazim* and the *Almandel* does not hold up under closer examination. There is no textual basis in *Sefer HaRazim* – either in the Hebrew or Latin versions – for associating the second heaven with Mercury. This correspondence originates with Ganell himself, not with the earlier *Sefer HaRazim*. As such, Gehr's reliance on Ganell's work does not reflect the earlier tradition she seeks to reconstruct, but rather a later Christian reception of it. The only shared element between *Sefer HaRazim* and the *Almandel* – the number twelve – reflects a widespread astrological motif rather than a meaningful structural parallel. Finally, the authors' claims for a "Jewish phase" in the transmission of the *Almandel* can be more plausibly explained by its attribution to King Solomon, a figure widely invoked in magical texts. As has been shown, such attributions often reflect imagined transmission histories rather than actual sources. For these reasons, Gehr's argument remains less convincing than its predecessors.

The question that remains is whether version F represents an Arabic prototype – a crucial issue, given that this version is often regarded as one of the earliest links in the chain that enabled "Arabic magic" to circulate in the Latin West. Before revisiting this argument in light of our examination of *The Seven Names*, it is worth summarizing what we know about version F, which is commonly believed to go back to an Arabic precursor, and reviewing the main indications for the existence of such a source.

I will focus here on the first work incorporated into the Florentine Codex, *The Book concerning the Almandal and its Operation*, which is generally considered the closest to the presumed Arabic original. There are

---

[143] Sofer, "Wearing God," 306 n. 7.

indeed several features within this work that seem to point to an Arabic source – features that Véronèse has listed. First, there are the onomastics: names and technical terms with Arabic morphology, transliterated into Latin, often in forms that are difficult to identify with certainty. Whether these result from the translator's choices or from subsequent scribes remains unclear. These include, most obviously, the term *mandel* itself, but also various spellings of the angel Michael (*Mahekil, Mahekeil*, etc.), and, most notably, the identification of the spiritual agents involved as djinns and *shayāṭīn* (devils, demons).[144] To this, we should add the broader context: *The Book concerning the Almandal and its Operation* appears within a codex that, as discussed earlier, also preserves works known to have been translated from Arabic. These elements provide substantial support for the view that we are dealing with a Latin translation of an Arabic work.

I do not seek to reject this possibility. Rather, I wish to offer a new perspective, based on the patterns that emerge when we compare *The Book concerning the Almandal and its Operation* to *The Seven Names*. In his study, Véronèse noted that reading through the *Almandal* text, one may well get the impression of a bricolage.[145] It seems that the instrument, the *almandel*, functions here as an organizing principle around which independent recipes, some resembling known talismanic practices,[146] have been gathered. While I have not found direct parallels for these recipes, it is possible that, as in *The Seven Names*, we are witnessing an effort to collect and reframe magical materials within a single, more systematic structure – in this case, one defined by the *almandel* as a ritual instrument. Is it possible that the object referred to here as the *almandel* received its name due to exposure to Arabic materials? Is it possible, then, that we are dealing with a work – as in the case of *The Seven Names* – in which Arabic sources were reworked and incorporated, but which does not necessarily represent a translation of a single Arabic (lost) prototype? If we consider the broader pattern and the very use of the term *almandel*, this possibility cannot be ruled out and deserves closer consideration.

The term *almandel* appears in many known Arabic and Persian works; however, based on the current state of research, none of these references seem to describe a metal (*almandel*) or wax (*almadel*) instrument of the kind found in the Latin versions. As Travis Zadeh argued, the ritual and content of the *mandal* (and thus the very term itself) were unstable.[147]

---

[144] Véronèse, *L'Almandal*, 16–18.
[145] Ibid., 23.
[146] Ibid., 28.
[147] Zadeh, "Postscript," 638–639.

He later invoked Malinowski's "coefficient of weirdness": *Mandal* works precisely because it is "estranging," a catch-all term for all these different shapes and rituals.[148] For example, the renowned historian Ibn Khaldūn refers to an *almandel* practice as a divinatory technique, specifically one involving catoptromancy: "In the towns, we find a group of people who strive to make a living out of (predicting the future), because they know that the people are most eager to know it. ... others make their predictions by looking into mirrors and into water. They are called 'drawers of circles' *(ḍārib al-mandal)*."[149]

This understanding of *mandal* as a magical circle used for catoptromancy or, more generally, harnessing demonic, angelic, or astral powers, was widespread, appearing in both Jewish and Islamic texts.[150] For example, one of the earliest Arabic accounts of the use of *mandal* appears in Abū ʿUthmān al-Jāḥiẓ's discussion on djinns, where it is mentioned as an instrument for controlling them.[151] During the eleventh century, Abū l-Faḍl Muḥammad al-Ṭabasī wrote on the *mandal* in his magic manual, treating it as a magical circle used to coerce demons and spirits.[152] In the twelfth century, the Jewish Gaon Shmuel ben Ali referred to *mandal* in his (Judeo-Arabic) treatise on the resurrection, describing it as a catoptromantic practice.[153] This association also appears in the mid-thirteenth century in *The Book of Charlatans*.[154] The connection between *mandal* and catoptromancy is further attested in magical recipes and manuals: A Judeo-Arabic recipe from the early sixteenth century describes a *"mandal* by cup,"[155] while another fifteenth-century Judeo-Arabic source employs a *mandal* to recover stolen items.[156] Even in contemporary practice, hydromancy is often referred to as

---

[148] Zadeh, "Tracing the Sorcerer's Circle," 96.
[149] Ibn Khaldūn, *The Muqaddimah*, II, 201.
[150] See, for example, the glossary in Dorpmüller, *Religiöse Magie*, 247; Nünlist, *Dämonenglaube im Islam*, 46 n. 22. The word *mandal* traces back to the Sanskrit *mandala*, as Pingree already suggested (in his "Learned Magic," 48). See also Zadeh, "Postscript," 628. For a recent and extensive discussion, see Zadeh, "Tracing the Sorcerer's Circle," 93–94.
[151] Zadeh, "Tracing the Sorcerer's Circle," 112–113.
[152] Zadeh, "Postscript," 632–633; Zadeh, "Tracing the Sorcerer's Circle," 97–98 and 124–129.
[153] Stroumsa, "Twelfth Century Concepts of Soul and Body," 319–321; Zadeh, "Tracing the Sorcerer's Circle," 103.
[154] Jawbarī, *The Book of Charlatans*, 229. Interestingly, Jawbarī dedicated a whole chapter to the deceptions of the Jews (chapter 5). Bosworth, after observing some signs of Jewish influence within the Banū Sāsān, cites this chapter as the sole substantial evidence for a Jewish presence in their ranks. See Bosworth, "Jewish Elements in the Banū Sāsān."
[155] Sofer, *Solomonic Magic*, chapter 14.
[156] Bohak, *A Fifteenth-Century Manuscript*, I, 199–200.

mandal.[157] In several cases, the *mandal* was understood not only as a space for divination but also as a device for trapping djinns, reflecting a broader perception of catoptromantic vessels as tools for spirit capture.[158]

An exception to these usages appears in Yemenite eighteenth-century texts, discovered and discussed by Anne Regourd, which circulated under the title *The Book of the Mandal of Solomon* (Kitāb al-Mandal al-Sulaymānī).[159] Rather than focusing on divination, summoning demons, or locating lost objects, these texts center on exorcism – specifically, identifying the possessing demon or demonic tribe and acting against it. This type of exorcistic practice is also attested in earlier Latin, Greek, Hebrew, aljamiado, and Armenian sources.[160] In the Yemenite texts, the *mandal* functions as a seal (or, in some cases, a "script") written on the door and on the floor, which is then shown to the demoniac during the ritual.[161]

Interestingly, a sixteenth- or seventeenth-century Judeo-Arabic recipe from the Cairo Genizah, examined by Dora Zsom, appears to share certain features with version F.[162] While some sections of this fragment, as Zsom demonstrates, parallel a seventeenth-century Arabic treatise published by Bonmariage and Moureau,[163] the specific recipe under discussion – found on folio 1v – does not. This recipe, incorporating both Islamic and Jewish elements, describes a method for seeking permission from the demons inhabiting the location where a magical operation is to be performed.[164] It instructs practitioners to place "a new white *mandal*" before them, seemingly referring to the magical circle used in catoptromancy.[165] Although this use of *mandal* differs from the context in version F, certain onomastic details in the recipe display morphological similarities to some of the *nomina* found in version F. For example, the

---

[157] Worrell, "Ink"; Fahd, *La divination arabe*, 49 n. 5. For a broader lexical discussion, see Hamès, "Mandalas," 157–158. See also Zadeh, "Tracing the Sorcerer's Circle." For a short discussion on the Latin *almandal*, see ibid., 103–104.

[158] Zadeh, "Postscript," 630–639.

[159] Regourd, "Al-Mandal as-sulaymānī appliqué." Regourd has found more (later) sources that contain such practice. See Regourd, "A Twentieth-Century Manuscript."

[160] Consider, for example, the *Testament of Solomon*. For the Armenian text, which seems to employ Arabic materials as well, see Macler, *L'enluminure arménienne profane*, 30–42. Interestingly, Macler has identified the common Arabic "string letters" as "caractères cabalistique"(!). For the aljamiado text, which Regourd also refers to, see Albarracín Navarro and Martínez Ruiz, *Medicina*.

[161] Regourd, "Al-Mandal as-sulaymānī appliqué," 142–143; Regourd, "Images de djinns," 262–263.

[162] Zsom, "A Judeo-Arabic Fragment."

[163] Bonmariage and Moureau, *Le Cercle des lettres de l'alphabet*.

[164] Zsom, "A Judeo-Arabic Fragment," 97.

[165] Ibid., 102.

variations *Sefectin*, *Sephetin*, *Sefeçin*, and others in version F[166] resemble the name *SFW'YN* preserved in the Genizah fragment.[167]

None of these sources refers to the *mandal* or *mandel* as the specific instrument described by the Latin texts, neither in terms of its physical description nor of its modus operandi. As we have seen, in the late Middle Ages, the term *mandal* generally refers to the practice itself (or the circle or script employed within it), rather than to the tablet described by the Latin works. The earliest mention of an *almandel* similar to the one in version F appears in William of Auvergne's *De legibus* in the thirteenth century, when the notion of *mandal* as a divinatory practice is already attested.

Significantly, the oldest manuscript of *De legibus* (thirteenth century) preserves marginal annotations that shed light on contemporary understandings of the *almandel*. As Boudet has observed, in the margin where William mentions the *almandel*, a note reads: "This figure of the *mandal* or *almandel* is to be prayed to and venerated, and especially the mirror of Apollo, in which they are inserted to give responses."[168] It appears that this medieval Latin reader – whose hand is likely contemporary with, if not identical to, that of the main scribe – associated the *almandel* with catoptromancy (the "mirror of Apollo") and with a vessel used to imprison spirits for divinatory purposes, rather than with the physical instrument described in version F.[169] The *almandel* described in version F (and echoed in William of Auvergne's *De legibus*) appears to be an exceptional reworking of the otherwise fluid *mandal* tradition that Zadeh has charted.[170] Although a *mandal* could designate many kinds of ritual diagrams or spaces, no extant Latin, Arabic, or Judeo-Arabic source has yet been shown to describe this particular portable altar. In short, this *almandel* sits outside the range of *mandal* variants currently documented.

Although the *almandel* as an altar of the kind described in version F is not clearly attested in medieval sources available to us today – rendering definitive conclusions impossible – Regan's discovery of the *areola*, and the fact that such an altar is mentioned in various Latin works from at least the thirteenth century, leave open the possibility that version F represents an attempt to incorporate a Christian instrument into a text that also draws on Arabic formulas. The naming of this instrument as

---

[166] Véronèse, *L'Almandal*, 25–26.
[167] Zsom, "A Judeo-Arabic Fragment," 115.
[168] The Latin is transcribed by Boudet, *Entre science et nigromance*, 217 n. 45.
[169] On the mirror of Apollo, which William also mentioned, see Delatte, *Catoptromancie grecque*, 18–19.
[170] Zadeh, "Tracing the Sorcerer's Circle."

almandel may reflect a similar strategy to that seen in *The Seven Names*, where attributing authorship to a Muslim figure lent the work the prestige and authority associated with Islamic scholarship. The word *mandel* may therefore have been adopted simply as a prestigious, exotic label – evoking the well-known magical term – for a Christian ritual instrument that had been supplemented with Arabic-derived formulas.[171] Put differently, the use of *mandel* in version F may reflect the scribe's choice to frame a culturally mixed device in recognizably Arabic terms, without necessarily pointing to a lost Arabic exemplar. As Zadeh aptly wrote:

> The charge of the "foreign" sticks, for there is much truth behind it, as large-scale group formations and ideologies are hybrid by nature, products of mixed parentage. Much of the conceptual vocabulary and epistemic power of the occult sciences are indeed born of exotic origins. ... the *mandal*, which Ṭabasī and others use as a term of art for the sorcerer's circle, can be traced to the Sanskrit *maṇḍala*, signifying both circle and realm.[72]

My argument, however, does not fully explain the term *areola* in the Latin text. Considering Regan's description of the *areola* as a "portable altar" – an interpretation that was also adopted by Christian practitioners who explicitly called the *almadel* an "altar of consecration" – it is reasonable to suspect that the choice of *areola* was intended to evoke an altar-like object.[173] One possibility, though not without its difficulties, is that *areola* may have been understood as a diminutive of *ara* ("altar"), formed with the suffix *-ola*.[174] This still leaves unexplained the shift from *ara* to *are*,[175] as well as the fact that the common diminutive for altar in Latin is *arula*. The choice of *areola*, then, is unusual. Nevertheless, morphologically, *areola* remains closer to *arula* than to *almadel* (or *almandel*), suggesting that the term may have been selected for its Christian resonance rather than for any etymological connection to *almadel* – a term that may well have been unfamiliar to the author of *De coloribus et virtutibus lapidum*.

---

[171] In that sense, although *almandel* is a technical label rather than a personal name, it seems to perform (mutatis mutandis) the Foucauldian role of the author function, providing a unifying, authoritative tag that organizes otherwise heterogeneous material.

[172] Zadeh, "Postscript," 628.

[173] On the *almandel* being an altar, see Regan, "The De consecratione lapidum," 308. In Latin, *areola* usually refers to a small garden bed or a small open space (diminutive of *area*).

[174] An allomorph of *-ula*.

[175] It is tempting to interpret "are" as the plural of "ara" (arae) with the final "a" dropped – a practice commonly seen in plural forms in medieval Latin orthography. However, this explanation remains speculative.

In other words, I suggest that the Latin *almandel* could be a deliberate rebranding of the *areola*, the small, portable "altar of consecration" familiar to Latin Christianity. By attaching the Arabic-sounding name *almandel* to this recognizably Christian device, the compiler overlaid a Christian object with the aura of Islamicate magic. The result is a hybrid artifact: structurally an *areola*, terminologically a *mandal*, and ritually supplied with Arabic-derived invocations. This renaming strategy does not point to a lost Arabic prototype; rather, it shows how a Latin author appropriated the cachet of Arabic occult science to recast the small altar for a new (multicultural) magical context.[176] If this reading is correct, it invites us to reconsider the linear narrative in which an Arabic prototype was gradually Christianized into the Latin *Liber Intelligentiarum*, eventually shifting from a demonic to an angelic operation – a notion broadly accepted by scholars.

If my interpretation of the evidence is correct, it would not be the first instance in the Florentine Codex where Arabic materials are incorporated into texts that are not direct or complete translations of Arabic sources. Immediately following the *Almandel* texts in the codex is another Latin work, *Liber Bileth* (The Book of Bileth), discussed in the previous section. Like the *Almandel*, *Liber Bileth* aims to summon demons and subject them to the practitioner's will, incorporating passages drawn from Jewish Babylonian magical traditions.[177] The appearance of the Quranic figures Hārūt and Mārūt within this Latin text has led some scholars to posit the existence of an otherwise unknown Arabic source. However, it seems more plausible that these references entered the text through a later encounter with Arabic material. The authors of *Liber Bileth*, possibly like those behind *The Seven Names* or the *Almandel*, reworked materials from different languages – Aramaic, Hebrew, Judeo-Arabic, and Arabic – into a new composite treatise.

If this is the case, then the decision to refer to the Christian ritual object as *almandel* in version F may have been motivated less by direct translation from an Arabic source and more by the prestige associated with Islamic science – a pattern already observed in the cases of Geber and,

---

[176] This is not at all a unique strategy, even when it comes to the *mandal*. As Zadeh already noted ("Postscript," 632): "The power of the category lies not so much in its foreign origin, which can at once be divested of earlier associations and entirely repurposed in a new idiom through distinct practices and cosmological concerns. Rather, it is precisely the proven efficacy of these diagrams and the rituals associated with them that lends the *mandal* universal, scientific authority."

[177] Sofer, *Solomonic Magic*, chapter 8.

possibly, *The Seven Names*. Yet this strategy was not static. As historical and cultural contexts shifted, so too did the value attached to Arabic knowledge. When Arabic science began to lose its universal prestige, and was increasingly viewed, particularly in the Italian Renaissance, as partial, outdated, or even fraudulent, the incentive to attribute magical practices to an imaginary Arab sage diminished, though it did not disappear entirely. Indeed, we still find treatises on divination attributed to an Arab named Almadel.[178] Nevertheless, the growing distance from Arabic scientific authority is evident in Renaissance critiques of astrology and medicine, often dismissed as works filled with "fictions and superstitions."[179]

It is therefore unsurprising that an expanded version of the popular *Liber Intelligentiarum* no longer employs the term *almadel*. Possibly as part of a broader effort to reclaim and emphasize Jewish-Hebrew origins, a yet unstudied Hebrew text composed in Italy replaces the term *almadel* altogether, substituting it with *Yahilion* – a choice that underscores its distancing from earlier, Arabic-associated terminology:[180]

> The Book of *Yahilion* by Solomon, son of David, King of Israel, is divided into four parts. In the first part, it speaks of the altitudes of the East (and its altitudes are nine) and their powers. In the second, of the altitudes of the South, and its altitudes are five, and their powers. In the third, of the western altitudes, which are seven, and the northern altitudes, which are three, and their powers. In the fourth part, how [and] what this holy *Yahilion* does ...[181]

This discovery is significant for two main reasons. First, it reveals a previously unknown seventeenth-century Hebrew-Italian version of the *Liber Intelligentiarum*, which substitutes twenty-four altitudes for the customary twelve. Second, its title, which may derive from the combination of two divine names often engraved on the *almandel* (*Yah* and *Elion*), appears in inquisitorial records. This, I propose, allows us to identify a book mentioned by Barbierato as circulating in eighteenth-century Venice under the title *Santi Hoeleon Hipottum, Book of the Wisest King Solomon* (S. Hoeleon Hipottum Libro del sapientissimo re Salomone) with this

---

[178] Veenstra, "The Holy Almandal," 210–211.
[179] Hasse, *Success and Suppression*, 250–254.
[180] Cincinnati, Hebrew Union College Library, Ms. 562.
[181] Ibid., 1r:
ספר של יהאיליון משלמה בן דוד מלך ישראל, נחלק לד' חלקים. בחלק הראשון נדבר ממדרגות שהם לצד מזרח (וומדרגותיו תשעה) וכוחותיו. בשני במדרגות שהם לצד דרום, ומדרגותיו חמשה וכוחותיו. בשלישי במדרגות מערב שהם שבעה, ומדרגות צפון שהם שלשה וכוחותיהם. בחלק הרביעי איך מה יעשה יהאיליון הקדוש הזה

Hebrew-Italian *Liber Intelligentiarum*,[182] which notably omits any reference to an *almandel*.

This example illustrates the shifting dynamics surrounding the figure of the imagined Arab magician and how this construct shaped the texts under examination. It also underscores the importance of approaching such works with caution, particularly given the fragmentary state of the evidence. As with the well-known "Geber problem," it is important to acknowledge the inherent challenges – indeed, the *problem* – posed by texts that appear to stem from a now-lost source. While hypothesizing the existence of such a source remains a valid and sometimes necessary approach, alternative explanations remain possible.

The silence of the surviving sources does not necessarily imply the absence of such a tradition, and my analysis should not be read as an *argumentum ex silentio*. Rather, this examination suggests that caution is needed when assuming straightforward translations or the existence of prototypes in a milieu where texts were constantly reworked, adapted, and treated as open and fluid. Once this is recognized, new possibilities emerge, allowing alternative narratives and new hypotheses for the transmission and transformation of these works to be proposed.

Concluding Remarks

Building on recent scholarship, I suggest exercising added caution before classifying a Latin or Hebrew compilation that contains Arabic features as a work of "Arabic magic," implying that it is a product of a lost Arabic source. While certain medieval authors (like in the case of Geber) invoked an "Arab magician" to bolster authority, that attribution need not imply an Arabic prototype. Practitioners were often eager to associate their materials with an imagined Arab magician, whether this was based on direct or indirect contact with actual Arabic texts and practitioners, or entirely independent of them. Although current scholarship fully recognizes the complexity of medieval magical transmission, discussions sometimes fall back – explicitly or implicitly – on relatively linear scenarios that depend on sources not yet in evidence. Must *The Seven Names* be assigned to a specific wave of Arabic-to-Latin translation? Is the Christian *Almandel* intelligible only as a gradual reworking of an earlier Arabic prototype? How far can we describe any translation process when the presumed Vorlage is still

---

[182] Barbierato, *Nella stanza dei circoli*, 173–174.

hypothetical? The case studies in this Element reopen such questions and sketch alternative, plausible routes of compilation, borrowing, and rebranding that do not rely on a (single) lost original or prototype.

The Florentine Codex, which some have listed among works of Arabic-to-Latin translations, illustrates why alternative scenarios remain plausible. *The Seven Names*, edited and translated here in full, offers us a glimpse into how such processes may have been shaped by the specific historical, social, cultural, and intellectual context of its compiler(s). Whether this work originated in the thirteenth century or somewhat later, it clearly incorporates Jewish and Islamic materials, some of which parallel known Judeo-Arabic and Hebrew sources. These features, at the very least, question the possibility of an Arabic original translated into Latin.

I would like to reiterate that the current state of research on medieval Arabic magical works does not yet permit us to draw definitive conclusions. This is equally true for *The Book concerning the Almandal and its Operation*, although we can outline several possible explanations for its presence in the Florentine Codex. The widely accepted view sees it as a translation from a lost Arabic prototype into Latin during the thirteenth century – a reasonable and well-supported argument. Yet, based on external evidence and the analysis presented here, I propose an alternative possibility. This remains, of course, a hypothesis – one that will need to be refined and reexamined as research progresses and new sources emerge. In such discussions, the role of the imagined Arab magician – a figure whose presence in these texts may or may not reflect a genuine (whether direct or indirect) engagement with Arabic materials – should be considered. Recognizing this dynamic is essential for any attempt to reconstruct the complex history of these works and their transmission.

The notion of the imagined Arab magician is by no means unique within the landscape of the medieval and early modern periods. In certain cultural and historical contexts, Jews were similarly sought-after as purveyors of magical knowledge. Some Christian magical texts were attributed to figures such as Rabi[n] Abognazar (Figure 5),[183] or framed as Kabbalah to lend them an air of Jewish authority.[184] Such cases, as we saw, reflect a complex history of intercultural transmission, adaptation, and invention.

---

[183] Paris, Bibliothèque nationale de France, Français MS. 25314.
[184] London, Wellcome Collection, MS. 1432.

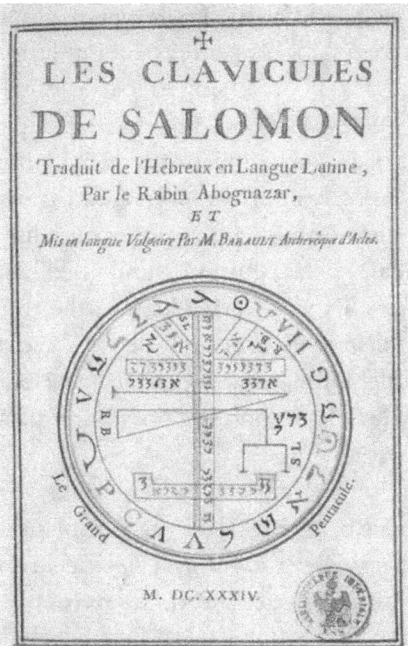

Figure 5 Abognazar's French *Clavicula Salomonis*.

Mindful that the absence of evidence cannot warrant definitive conclusions *ex silentio*, I have included here a complete edition and translation of *The Seven Names*. I hope that the appearance of this text – and future editions of other Latin magical works – will invite Arabists and other specialists to pursue comparative analyses that may substantiate, refine, or overturn the hypotheses set out in this study.

Appendix A

The Book of Seven Names: Edition

Florence, Biblioteca Nazionale Centrale, II.III.214, 38r–41r.

Symbols used in the edition:
< > – Editorial supplement.
(?) – Doubtful reading.
X[x] – An uncertain expansion of an abbreviated word.

§1 Dixit Muhamet filius Alhascen et filius Amoemen, et dixit Abnbeluer Hamet filius Habrae, et dixit Abubecher filius Mugehic, et dixit Abulacha Abdiram[en] filius Abduc, et dixit Abnbeluer Mauhmet filius Bosit, quod hec sunt nomina Dei VII secreta, secundum numerum VII dierum, per omne tempus discurrit. Et sunt VII circuli, super quorum singulum angelus unus constitutus est, qui cottidie Creatorem laudat cum nomine sibi deputato. Et sic fecit Deus VII celos et VII terras et VII maria, et ceteras creaturas per septenarium numerum disposuit sua mirabili virtute operante. Et sic unicuique VII dierum unum nomen sanctum et benedictum attribuit.

<The First Name – Saturday>
§2 Diei ergo Sabbati primum nomen et maximum concessit, per quod Dominis legem in monte Synay Moisi dedidit et in scripturis secretionibus ei ostendit, et operabatur per illud Moyses in omni quod volebat. Et cum hoc nomine orabat Moyses sumo[185] mane et vespere per unumquemque diem. Quicumque hoc nomen /38v/ sanctum sciverit vel secum habuerit, devote Creatorem adorare debet, nec eum inmundus tangat, sin autem ante diem mortis, ab angelo percutietur. Quicumque aliquod operare voluerit quod super nomine diei Sabbati pertimuerit,[186] scribat illud nomen secrete, corpore et habitu mundus, in pergameno algacel,[187] et fumigabitur de costo et thure. Sed in die ab omni cibo se alienum constituat, exceptis pane et aqua, et servet nomen sacrum, et sic ubicumque manserit vel intraverit, securus existat.

---

[185] *Sic. Lege*: summo.
[186] *Sic. Lege*: pertinuerit.
[187] As Burnett already noted, this is الغزال, *al-ġazāl*, gazelle. See Burnett, "Inscriptio," 318.

<The Second Name – Sunday>

§3 Nomen vero secundum ex VII nominibus scribi debet in die Solis, et hoc nomen positum est in 6 celo, et angelus eius in sexto celo, qui cum hoc nomine Creatorem adorat. Et qui vult hoc nomen scribere, per duos dies ieiunare debet, ita ut carnem non comedat nec aliquid quod ex sanguine exeat. In secundo vero die hic nomen scribat, corpore et habitu mundus. Primum se et locum in quo fuerit cum preciosis fumigationibus fumigando et proprietatem tematis determinando, et postea hoc nomen scribat in argilla non cocta, quo scripto in aqua deleatur. Quique ille portare debet, cuius tam scriptum est, vel aliter predicto nominis scripte in texta non cocta tollatur olla rudis et in calentes ponatur et super ignem bulliat. Et os olle cum testa scripta cohoperiatur, donec testa eadem bene coquatur. Testa vero cum alchafor[188] postea fumiganda est. Deinde testa super tectum illius, pro quo hec facta sunt, reponatur, et Creatoris potentia aperientur intendenti mira.

<The Third Name – Monday>

§4 Nomen vero tertium, quod benedictum est et super celum V positum est, diei Lune atribuitur.[189] In pergameno de algacel scribi debet cum tincta de seue[190] facta et cafaram,[191] que duo marasi[192] debent cum mauard[193] et alcofor proprietate, cum nomine in eadem carta scribendo, quod et in omnibus nominibus intelligendum est. Hoc alias nomen praeest vias transgredientibus et mare intereuntibus vel transfretantibus et mercatoribus, quia omnes huius negotii in omne quod huius rei intendens voluerit, ei subitietur.

<The Fourth Name – Tuesday>

§5 Nomen autem quartum diei Martis deputatur, quod similiter cum sanguine columbe in pergameno tenuissimo atque mundo scribi debet. Quod cum scriptum fuerit, ponatur in olla vitrea illa carta et bene cohoperiatur. Hiis peractis, olla sublimine porte illius cui amor dari intenditur subhumanda est. Hoc enim nomen amori et dilectioni praeest, sed maxime muliebri. Sed cavendum est, ne hoc nomen alicui Deum non timenti nec ostendatur.

---

[188] From الكافور, *al-kāfūr*, camphor.
[189] *Sic. Lege*: attribuitur.
[190] Burnett has identified this as alum (from شب, *šabb*). See Burnett, "Inscriptio," 319.
[191] Burnett has identified this as saffron (from زعفران, *zafarān*). See ibid.
[192] From مرهم, *marham*, ointment?
[193] From ماء ورد, *māʾ ward*, rose water.

‹The Fifth Name – Wednesday›

§6 Nomen vero V die Mercurii ‹space› conceditur, in hoc enim die nomen V scribitur, eorum nomina quorum abhominationem volueris. Cum abhominationis oratione in eadem carta scribende erunt. Hiis ita que scriptis, carta subfumigabitur cum alhait[194] aut imasac.[195] Et hec carta in pergameno mundo scribenda est, quam mira sequentur.

‹The Sixth Name – Thursday›

§7 Nomen VI in die iovis scribetur, quod et in pelle de sucues[196] scribi debet, et postea duplicabitur carta et fumigabitur cum colubris[197] capite vel eius limgua.[198] Quibus peractis, actor, quando invisibilter incedere voluerit, prefectam cartam secum teneat. Et in nocte diem precedente, in quo hec tractare voluerit, nichil aliud com-/39r/-edat nisi panem açimum[199] cum olivis vel oleo. Et si ante regem intraverit, honorabit eum. Et cum munditia fiat.

‹The Seventh Name – [Friday]›

§8 Nomen vero VII cum ovo ‹space› suscitabat mortuos, et mutos et leprosos sanabat. Ultimo celo constitutum, quod in pergameno de areignum[200] scribere debet et suffumigabitur cum alood[201] ascaradal[202] rubeo sive glauco. Sed hoc nomen maxime muliebri amori conceditur, et per hec mulierem quamlibet a loco in quo fuerit ad locum libitum amoris tam provocari poterit. Et cavendum est, ne peccati causa fiat.

‹The Exorcism of the First Name›

§9 Hic est exorçismus primi nominis, cum quo illud nomen exorçiçari debet. Deus, qui cum tua sapientia et tua virtute super gentes, et cum tuo nomine, magnum exaltatum datorem, et unam[203] mundum, maximo honorato sacro, quod super illa nomina honorasti incomprehensibilia veridica ex alta maxima, te supliciter invoco, ut meum tema ad effectum perducas. Hac oratione invocata et in carta ista scripta, cum nomine proprio nomen proprium tematis dicendum est et in carta scribendum. Hoc

---

[194] Possibly from حلتيت, *ḥiltīt*, asafoetida.
[195] Possibly from مصطكى, *muṣṭakā*, mastic.
[196] Possibly from the Latin *sciurus*, squirrel.
[197] *Sic. Lege*: colubri.
[198] *Sic. Lege*: lingua.
[199] *Sic. Lege*: azymum.
[200] Possibly from الغنم, *al-ġanam*, [the] sheep.
[201] From العود, *al-ʿūd*, [the] aloe.
[202] From الصندل, *aṣ-ṣandal*, [the] sandalwood.
[203] *Sic. Lege*: unum.

autem sciendum: quod, antequam hoc nomen scribatur, actor tribus diebus corpore et habitu mundus ieiunet, cavendo ne causam peccati faciat. Et post invocationem scriptam, hii anuli scribendi erunt. Et quicumque hoc nomen sanctum scribit, munditia et ieiunio completis, tunc nominet discipulos triplicitatis presentis et solem et ventos qui huic triplicitati pertinent, et fumigent[204] nomen scriptum cum fructum[205] sandali et sandalo, et invocabit Creatorem per hoc nomen de omni eo quod voluerit. Sed cavendum ne aliquis illud habeat nec sciat, nisi iuste illud tractaverit. Et cum scribit nomina ventorum in loco suo, scribantur et nomina stellarum et nomen proprium tematis et nomina angelorum triplicitatis presentis in loco suo. Et postea nomen prefatum cum hoc exorçismo exorçiçari debent,[206] et cartam hanc secum habere debet, et humiliabit se ille quem queris, id est pro cuius causa cartam fecisti. Quam cum hoc nomine Coueida regen[207] Aron in aurorum,[208] qui victum tenebat in tantum ut ei, quem captivaverat Haaron rex in omnibus obsequebatur. Et hoc nomen Algorismus, philosophus quidam et astrologus, Coueide captivo atribuit,[209] cum omni eo quod nomini neccesarium fuit. Huius autem nominis effectus mirabilis est, si ea que sunt neccesaria non minuantur.

<The Exorcism of the Name – Agion>
§10 Hic est exorçismus servi nominis Agion:[210] <space> Karome Ascfelan L'ue H'etes Cefelam K'ete Isctedhene H'edecerie L'uede Midha Faytes Midha Iuri Berete Cutas Autunas Resce Uijuim Tudhylu[m] Tiris Heili Buraliburab H'esec Mesete[m] Kelietinet H'eremecheri Aeliet Terh'erh'e.

<The Exorcism and Uses of the Third Name>
§11 Quando nomen tertium scripseris et suffumigaveris, et illud cum illis que sunt sibi necessaria tractaveris, exorçiçabis illud cum hoc exorçimus: Ane Adonay Jelohim Jeloy Ebraym et Ysaach et Israel Uueiloy Moyse Uuaharon Uueyloy Siulle Anabim et Myrus Ertof Erte Uesceley K'eilen Brenis Metihcile Ancu Symenac Dauiari Amacye Beuyaium /39v/ Adonay Bamar Esloy Ydi Ydda Jeahalum et Deburbulohhun Abda Moyse Uahhol Batunamehun Uuefalel Faed Debir Uuebrai Uuelubabi Duth Uuetham Unet Adonay Iabieth Tumaete Uuascelcy Leyk'e Bunekale Uehuuegale

---
[204] *Sic. Lege*: fumiget.
[205] *Sic. Lege*: fructibus.
[206] *Sic. Lege*: debet.
[207] *Sic. Lege*: regens.
[208] *Sic. Lege*: auroram.
[209] *Sic. Lege*: attribuit.
[210] From Ἅγιον, holy.

Imilxate Uemes Cetrethe Iedha Mebahsol'ia Udenaora Amisere Uueh'scy Mehehtuete et Danie Uuethdimine Methe Adde Maichxcein Uueema Hal'um Mallxhim Ieib K'hohmethe Lethalxmin Uuemandaya Lyeydaa Bieteuuete Uues Celey Cyhcebyahbismay Cileihce Ie Ie Ie Ie Ie Ie Adonay Sabaoth Ioseph Hahcarubin Isodey Ahue Asyrahie Uuecescelc H'edhalrean Rabhen Intexe Feley Me Bunexch'xi. De omni quod in mente habeo, michi faciatis et compleatis, et quod capiat me cor et anima illius N., filie illius N., ut ei N. in omnibus que voluerit obsequatur. Hiisque dictis nominabis quos volueris, et postea dices: Nominavi te Creatorem et nominavi tuos angelos, et mea crudelitas[211] in te solo est. Et sicut tu es Creator, in te tota mente confido et in tua virtute et in tuis sanctissimis angelis benedictis et tibi ministrantibus in tuis celis: Zendi, Bu^{n}di, Sereintudi, Jehuelme, Leysxe. Et vobis me comendo cum istis nominatis nominibus, ut pro me pie rogetis in mei tematis proficere, quod michi serviat cor illius N. filia illius N. Et postea: Rogo vos, Michael, Uuobriel, Uu'emitaiel, Ueronsiale, et rogo vos, Gahahos, Zachare, Iaichel, Uefahos, et adiuvetis Zrareiaiel, Uefahos, et adiuvetis[212] in eo opere, sicut vobis precepit benedictus et exaltatus, et ut mandatum meum ad effectum perducatis cum Dei gratiarum benedictione. Quicumque istam cartam scripserit secundum quod dictum est et eius percepta servaverit vel compleverit et in vase argenteo eam posuerit, vase cum preciosis speciebus intus et extra peruncto, quando regem aloqui[213] voluerit, per factum vas cum carta et in sinu teneat. Et aliud, si forte in bello adiuverit, nichil timebit. Et si in die Alcoara[214] hoc nomen scriptum fuerit secundum quod dictum est, ut per illud mulier ad amorem provocetur, confidenter artem tractet et sic propositum ad effectum perducet.

<The Exorcism and Uses of the Fourth Name>
§12 Cum ergo nomen 4 scripseris, exorçiçabis illud cum hoc exorçismo tribus vicibus, postquam per tres dies continuos ante ieiunabis et balneabis omni die semel. Et debet scribi hoc nomen de zafaran optimo et musco et alood raptab (?),[215] et fumigabis illud cum alood et temiem,[216] si Deus voluerit. Et exorçismus est iste, dices: Bisam Yley Eulu^m Escelectu^m Uuaet Epyleicum Je angeli Dei benedicti mundi totius amen. Et hec sunt vestra nomina: Holnuchie Egra Unct Aruaheceh Basahin Angu Uuetel

---
[211] *Sic. Lege*: credulitas.
[212] Dittography of "Zachare, Iaichel, Uefahos, et adiuvetis"?
[213] *Sic. Lege*: alloqui.
[214] From الزهرة, *az-zuhara*, Venus. That is, Friday.
[215] From رطب, *raṭb*, that is, fresh aloe?
[216] From θυμίαμα, *thumiama*, incense.

Mehil Scellim L'eli Acimaleycum. Cum istis sanctis nominibus in corona Creatoris scriptis, ut mittatis amorem in cor et animam illius N. filie N.

<The Exorcism and Uses of the Fifth Name>
§13 Iste est exorçismus in quo istud n<o>men V exorçiçari debet, postquam scriptum fuerit cum illis que ei neccesaria sunt, et fumigabis eum cum fumigatione precipua. Deus, per contorre,[217] tu es Deus solus, unus, potens, maximum, benedictus, lumen celi et terre, omnem secretorum scientiam pernoscens et magnum testimonium et exaltatum. Tu vero omnem tristitiam cordis aufers, et tu es gloriosus /40r/ et dator ut meum propositum ad effectum perducas, et hiis dictis nominabis quod volueris et quem quesieris. Et antequam hoc nomen scribatur, necesse est auctorem per unum diem ieiunare, et in balneo mundissime declarare,[218] et mundos pannos vestire, et postea locum mundissimum introire. Et sit solus, et fiet eius voluntas.

<The Exorcism of the Sixth Name>
§14 Iste est exorçismus huius nominis 6 <space> quem legere debes et super hoc nomen, postquam scriptum fuerit: Bis Mellah Uuebile Uueraot Uuremich'l' Uuescerafil et angelos benedictos, qui nec comedunt nec bibunt, quoniam eorum cibus est benedictio et eorum potus orationes sunt. Sua capita in celis sunt, et eorum pedes fines et terminos terre tangunt, et eorum alle[219] orientem et occidentem tangunt.

<The Exorcism and Uses of the Seventh Name>
§15 Et iste est exorçismus huius nominis VII, cum quo hoc nomen, postquam scriptum fuerit, exorçiçari debet. Et sit in die Veneris: ille qui trahit ventos de locis suis et nubes de suis terminis, et qui mare Moysi apperuit. Et ille qui salvavit Habraam amicum exaltatum et datorem et Creator honoratus rex. Per hec benedicta nomina et magne exaltata maxima completa, te rogo ut meum propositum ad effectum perducas. Hec autem res magne rei muliebri pertinet, qui[220] ad hoc nomen diei Veneris attribuitur. Et scribe hoc nomen cum uncto de elgule,[221] id est margaritas, et cafor,[222] id est camfora, et fumigabis eum cum alanbar,[223]

---

[217] *Sic. Lege*: percontor te.
[218] *Sic*. I translated it in the sense of "to make [the body] clear [of impurity]."
[219] *Sic. Lege*: ale.
[220] *Sic. Lege*: que.
[221] Burnett identified this as اللؤلؤ, *al-luʾluʾ*, pearl. See Burnett, "Inscriptio," 321 n. 29.
[222] See n. 187.
[223] From العنبر, *al-ʿanbar*, amber. On this name, which was used to refer to more than one specific substance, see Lev and Amar, *Practical Materia Medica*, 331 n. 47.

id est musco, et meuaro, id est aq[ua]ro[sae].²²⁴ Et in suffumigatione tene cartam super ignem, et postea in radio solis suspendatur. Et tene cum²²⁵ tecum in cingulo tuo aptatum, quin mulier nec puella postea, cum te viderit, statim in tuo amore non ardeat. Et si hoc nomen, secundum quod predictum est, et nomen alicuius mulieris in carta scriptum fuerit, nullo modo tuo amori resistere poterit.

<*Preliminary Requirements and The Book of Heh'eben son of Joseph*>
§16 Hic nominatur hora et dies secundum quas anni triplicitates dividuntur. Quicumque ergo aliquod istorum nominum predictorum scribere voluerit, in primis scire debet quomodo se huic artificio aptcet et cum illis omnibus que huic magisterio necessaria sunt. Et est iste liber de Heh'eben filii Iosep, maximi sapientis, et per hanc scientiam divinam sciebat annos siccos et humidos. In primis necesse est te per spatium trium dierum balneo declarare et cum carnali cibo abstinere. Post tres dies te fumigabis preciosis fumis et unguentis unges et panis²²⁶ mundissimis indues, et postea incipe quod vis istorum nominum scribere secundum thematis proprietatem, et erit quod vis.

<*General Instructions – The Second Name – Sunday*>
§17 Dies in quibus nomina scribuntur hec nominantur. Cum ergo vis aliquid adversus regem operari in die Solis et eius hora, nomen secundum scribendum est, et cum eo anuli²²⁷ secundi nominis, et exorçiçabis cum exorçismo sibi pertinente. Hiis itaque peractis, fumigetur carta cum fumigationibus sibi necessariis, ut supra diximus, et operabis postea sicut diximus. Et erit necesse te scire nomina triplicitatis et angelos, quorum ordine disponuntur tempora, et nec debes aliquid operari antequam scias nomina angelorum. Et debes scire nomina venti cuiusque triplicitatis et nomina stellarum et²²⁸ diversis triplicitatibus, et sic intelliges.

<*General Instructions – The Third Name – Monday*>
§18 /40v/ Nomen vero diei Lune scribi debet ad omne id quod volueris in die Lune et eius hora, et est nomen tertium. Et cum eo eius anulos et exorçiçabis suo exorçismo, et nichil de suo pretermittes. Et debes scire in qua triplicitate sis.

---

²²⁴ The manuscript reads "id est aqro," in an abbreviated form. Since the Arabic word seems to derive from ماء ورد, *mā' ward*, rose water, I interpreted it as aqua rosae.
²²⁵ *Sic*.
²²⁶ *Sic. Lege*: pannis.
²²⁷ *Sic. Lege*: anulum.
²²⁸ *Sic. Lege*: in.

<General Instructions – The Fourth Name – Tuesday>
§19 Nomen diei Martis causa belli scribitur cum omni eo qui nominavimus de suo in die Martis et eius hora. Debes scire triplicitatem quartam et nomina angelorum et stellarum et ventorum illius triplicitatis, in eris. Et scribe anulos huius et exorçiça, et non eris victus habente te nomen.

<General Instructions – The Fifth Name – Wednesday>
§20 Quintum nomen est die Mercurii. Quandoque ergo facultatem absconsam invenire voluerit, nomen 5 scribat in die Mercurii et eius hora, et anulos et exorçiçet et secum teneat, et per hec sciet si facultas alicui recondita est.

<General Instructions – The Sixth Name – Thursday>
§21 Iovis diei nomen prefectis et iudicibus pertinet, si in mente fuerit aliquod iudicium. Et hoc nomen est sextum, quod cum suis anulis scribendum et exorçiçandum, te corpore et habitu existente mundo. Et scribatur hoc nomen in die Iovis et eius hora, et nomen triplicitatis in quo fueris. Cum ergo iudicium introieris, hoc nomen tecum scriptum habeas.

<General Instructions – The Seventh Name – Friday>
§22 Nomen die[229] Veneris, causa amoris, ut te illa sequatur, in die Veneris et eius hora scribitur, et ei anuli[230] et exorçismus, <et> proprietatem tematis determinando, quod in omnibus intelligendum est. Et nominabis triplicitatem pertinentem diei, et fumigabis cum precibus et fumis suis. Et cum hoc nomine nomen illius quam queris scribatur.

<On The Names of the Angels and the Triplicities>
§23 De nominibus angellorum[231] custodientium anni tempora dicendum est. Deus benedictus primum temporis ver appellavit, secundum estatem, tertium auptumnum, quartum yemem, et unicuique tres menses atribuit, unicuique triplicitati angelum, et unicuique angelo tres angelos alios adiutores, et omni mensi unum angelum, qui in suo mense proprio suo domino serviat. Sciendum est ergo quod, quando aliquid huius rei operari vis, triplicitatem in qua fueris cognoscere debes, et nomen sui angeli, et mensem, et eius angelum, et nomen venti illius triplicitatis, et nomen stellarum eiusdem. Hiis ita computatis, nomen triplicitatis cum nominibus suorum angelorum, et nomen venti cum nominibus stellarum, et per nomen Dei magnum, quod est unum ex VII nominibus secundum rationem

---

[229] *Sic. Lege*: diei.
[230] *Sic. Lege*: eius anulos.
[231] *Sic.*

predictam, et iuranda erunt, ut rema ad effectum perducatur. Quibus peractis, votum intendentis potentia Creatoris complebitur.

<The Four Triplicities>
§24 Prima triplicitas a XXIIII^{or} die Martii usque ad XXIIII^{or} Iunii. Secunda ab illo die usque ad XXIIII^{or} Septembris. Tertia ab illo usque ad XXIIII^{or} Decembris. Quarta ab illo usque ad XXIIII^{or} Martii. Et hec est divisio anni per quatuor triplicitates, et invenies quod volueris de nominibus angelorum prime triplicitatis.

<The Lords of the Four Triplicities>
§25 Primus dominus orientis Daniel nuncupatur; eius vero ministri /41r/ ita dicuntur Dargimuail Egirmail Scagiail. Secunde triplicitatis dominus, qui et occidenti preest, dicitur Hardiail; huius autem discipuli Gibreta Gabil, L'imisciail, Sareil. Tertia triplicitatis dominis, qui est meridianus, dicitur Anail; eius socii Farany, Uthiail, Tagilalul. Quarte dominus, qui est septentrionalis, dicitur Szadfiail; eius socii Girmichael, Himiail, Firgiail.

<The Names of the Four Winds in Each Triplicity>
§26 Ventus orientalis in prima triplicitate dicitur Al'udum, in secunda K'edijah, in tertia Ehesrit, in quarta ventus de terra Mehhadⁱ. Ventus occidentis in prima triplicitate Amuuueea, in secduna M^{en}bor, in 3^a Mehaszor, in quarta Mam^{en}. Ventus meridiei in prima triplicitate Mesycur, in secunda Szaramir, in tertia Lak'or, in quarta Adyrayodu^m. Ventus septentrionalis in prima triplicitate Tahir, in secduna Aiaurmeniarobebenete, in tertia K'asur In^mazdeabesze, in quarta Gmadur.

<The Names of the Sun in Each Triplicity>
§27 Nomen solis in prima triplicitate Iebahor, in secunda Aichhim, in 3^a Uik'alul' Szimich, in quarta Agadhe.

<The Names of the Moon in Each Triplicity>
§28 Nomen lune in prima triplicitate Szeenisze, in secunda Aichhim, in tertia Iuk'al, in quarta Gerehe.

<The Seven Angels of the Weekdays>
§29 Nomen quoque angeli prime ferie Rosiael, secunde Gabriael, tertie Sumuael, quarte Michael, quinte Szadsiael, sexte Dimuael, septime K'iszsiael.

<General Instruction – The Angel of the Day>
§30 Sciendum vero quod, cum aliquid operari volueris, nomen angeli diem in quo fueris custodientis, cum Dei magno nomine eidem diei pertinente, scribi debet. Et in nominum promissorum invocatione habita, nomen euisdem angeli non taceatur.

Appendix B

The Book of Seven Names: Translation

§1 Muḥammad, son of Alhascen and son of Amoemen, said, and Abnbeluer Hamet, son of Habrae, said, and Abubecher, son of Mugehic, said, and Abulacha Abdiramen, son of Abduc, said, and Abnbeluer Mauhmet, son of Bosit, said that these are the seven secret names of God, according to the number of the seven days, <which> all time runs through. And there are seven circles, over each of which one angel is appointed, who praises the Creator every day with the name assigned to him. And thus, God made seven heavens and seven earths and seven seas, and arranged the rest of the creatures according to the number seven by the operation of His marvelous power. And so, to each of the seven days, He attributed one sacred and blessed name.

<The First Name – Saturday>
§2 Thus, He granted the first and greatest name to Sabbath, through which the Lord gave the Law to Moses on Mount Sinai and revealed to him in the secrets of the scriptures, and Moses performed all that he desired through it. And with this name, Moses prayed at the break of dawn and in the evening, every single day. Whoever has known or carried this holy name must worship the Creator devoutly, and let not the unclean touch it; but if he does so, he will be struck down by an angel before the day of <his> death. Whoever wishes to perform something that will have pertained to the name of the Sabbath day, let him write that name secretly, <being> clean in body and clothing, on parchment of gazelle, and it will be fumigated with costus oil and frankincense. But on <that> day, he should set himself apart from all food except for bread and water, and he should preserve the sacred name. And thus, wherever he stays or enters, he will be safe.

<The Second Name – Sunday>
§3 The second name of the seven names must be written on the day of the sun, and this name is placed in the sixth heaven, and its angel is in the sixth heaven, who, with this name, adores the Creator. And whoever wishes to write this name must fast for two days, so that he does not eat meat nor anything that comes from blood. On the second day, he should write this

name, <being> clean in body and clothing. First, he must fumigate himself and the place where he is with precious fumigations and determine the property of the subject, and afterward, he should write this name on unbaked clay, which, once written, should be erased in water. The one for whom it has been written must carry it, or alternatively, with the said written name on unbaked pottery, let an unused pot be taken, and let it be placed into the hot <coals>, and let it boil over the fire. And let the mouth of the pot be covered with the written shard until this shard is well baked. Afterward, the shard must be fumigated with camphor. Then let the shard be placed on the roof of the one for whom these things have been done, and by the power of the Creator, wonders will be revealed to the one who understands.

<The Third Name – Monday>
§4 The third name, which is blessed and placed above the fifth heaven, is attributed to the day of the moon. It must be written on parchment of gazelle with ink made of alum and saffron, which are two *marasi* that must <be mixed?> with the quality of rose water and camphor, with the name to be written on the same sheet, which must also be discerned for all the names. This other name presides over those crossing roads and those who become lost in the sea, or crossing it, and merchants, because everything of this matter, everything that one wishes to seek in this thing, will be supplied to him.

<The Fourth Name – Tuesday>
§5 The fourth name is assigned to the day of Mars, which likewise must be written with the blood of a dove on a very fine and clean parchment. When it has been written, let that sheet be placed in a glass jar and well covered. Once these things have been completed, the jar must be buried beneath the threshold of the gate of the one to whom love is sought to be given. For this name presides over love and affection, but especially of womanly <love>. But one must beware lest this name be shown to someone <who> does not fear God.

<The Fifth Name – Wednesday>
§6 The fifth name is granted on the day of Mercury, for on this day, the fifth name is written, along with the names of those whose abomination you wish for. With the prayer of abomination, they must be written on the same sheet. Once these have been written, the sheet will be fumigated with *alhait* or *imasac*. And this sheet must be written on clean parchment, upon which marvelous things will follow.

<The Sixth Name – Thursday>

§7 The sixth name shall be written on the day of Jupiter, and it must also be written on the skin of *sucues*, and afterward the sheet will be divided[232] and fumigated with the head of a snake or its tongue. When these have been completed, the practitioner, when he wishes to walk invisibly, should keep the designated sheet with him. And on the night before the day on which he wishes to perform, let him eat nothing else except unleavened bread with olives or oil. And if he enters before the king, he will honor him. And let it be done with cleanliness.

<The Seventh Name – [Friday]>

§8 The seventh name <shall be written> with an egg, <and> it resurrected the dead, and healed the mute and the leprous. It has been set up in the highest heaven, and it must be written on parchment of *areignum* and suffumigated with aloe and red or white sandalwood. But this name is especially granted to womanly love, and through these things, any woman can be summoned for love from the place where she may have been to a chosen place. And one must beware lest it be done for the sake of sin.

<The Exorcism of the First Name>

§9 This is the exorcism of the first name, with which that name must be exorcized: "O God, who, with Your wisdom and Your power over the nations, and with Your name, the great exalted giver, <who created> a world, the greatest, honored and sacred, which You have honored above those incomprehensible, true names, from the highest greatness, I humbly invoke You, so You may bring my matter to accomplishment." When this prayer has been invoked and written on this sheet, together with the proper name, the proper name of the matter must be spoken and written on the sheet. This, however, must be known: Before this name is written, the practitioner must fast for three days, being clean in body and clothing, <and being> careful not to commit sin. And after the invocation has been written, these rings must be written. And whoever writes this sacred name with purity and complete fasting, should then name the disciples of the present triplicity, and the sun, and the winds that belong to this triplicity, and he should fumigate the written name with sandal fruit and sandalwood, and he should invoke the Creator by this name for everything he wishes. But care must be taken so that no one else possesses or knows it, unless they have used it justly. And when he writes the names of the winds in their proper place, let the names of the stars, the proper name of the matter,

---

[232] From *duplicabitur*, which can also mean "will be duplicated."

and the names of the angels of the present triplicity also be written in their proper place. And afterward, the aforementioned name must be exorcized with this exorcism, and he must have this sheet with him, and he whom you seek will humble himself, that is, to the one for whose sake you made the sheet. When Coueida <bore> this name <against> King Aron in the East, who had been holding him subdued, <it was brought> to such a point that King Haaron, who had captured him, had now obeyed him in all things. And a certain Algorismus, a philosopher and astrologer, attributes[233] this name to the captive Coueida, with everything that was necessary for the name. And the effect of this name is miraculous if the necessary things are not diminished.

<The Exorcism of the [Second?] Name>
§10 This is the exorcism of the servant of the name Agion: <space> Karome Ascfelan L'ue H'etes Cefelam K'ete Isctedhene H'edecerie L'uede Midha Faytes Midha Iuri Berete Cutas Autunas Resce Uijuim Tudhylum Tiris Heili Buraliburab H'esec Mesetem Kelietinet H'eremecheri Aeliet Terh'erh'e.

<The Exorcism and Uses of the Third Name>
§11 When you have written the third name and suffumigated it, and when you have handled it with those things that are necessary for it, you shall exorcize it with this exorcism: Ane Adonay Jelohim Jeloy Ebraym and Ysaach and Israel Uueiloy Moyse Uuaharon Uueyloy Siulle Anabim et Myrus Ertof Erte Uesceley K'eilen Brenis Metihcile Ancu Symenac Dauiari Amacye Beuyaium Adonay Bamar Esloy Ydi Ydda Jeahalum and Deburbulohhun Abda Moyse Uahhol Batunamehun Uuefalel Faed Debir Uuebrai Uuelubabi Duth Uuetham Unet Adonay Iabieth Tumaete Uuascelcy Leyk'e Bunekale Uehuuegale Imilxate Uemes Cetrethe Iedha Mebahsol'ia Udenaora Amisere Uueh'scy Mehehtuete and Danie Uuethdimine Methe Adde Machxcein Uueema Hal'um Mallxhim Ieib K'hohmethe Lethalxmin Uuemandaya Lyeydaa Bieteuuete Uues Celey Cyhcebyahbismay Cileihce Ie Ie Ie Ie Ie Ie Adonay Sabaoth Ioseph Hahcarubin Isodey Ahue Asyrahie Uuecescelc H'edhalrean Rabhen Intexe Feley Me Bunexch'xi. May you do and complete for me everything that I have in mind, and may the heart and soul of that N., daughter of that N., capture me, so that she may accommodate N., in all the things that he/she desires. And having said these things, you will name those you wish, and afterward, say: I have called you Creator, and I have called Your angels,

---
[233] Another possibility: Algorismus bestows this name to the captive.

and my belief is in you alone. And just as You are the Creator, I trust in You with my whole mind, and in Your power, and in Your most sacred and blessed angels and those who serve You in Your heavens: Zendi, Bundi, Sereintudi, Jehuelme, Leysxe. And I entrust myself to you all with these named names, so that you may piously pray for me to benefit in my matter that the heart of that N., daughter of that N., may serve me. And afterward: I ask you, Michael, Uuobriel, Uu'emitaiel, Ueronsiale, and I ask you, Gahahos, Zachare, Iaichel, Uefahos, and <that> you assist Zrareiaiel, Uefahos, and <that> you assist in that work, just as the Blessed and Exalted One has commanded you, so that you may bring my command to accomplishment with the blessing of the graces of God. Whoever will have written this sheet, as has been said, and will have observed or completed its instructions, and will have placed it in a silver vessel, a vessel that has been anointed with precious spices inside and outside, when he has wished to address the king, let him hold the prepared vessel with the sheet in a pocket.[234] And furthermore, if by chance it will be useful in war, he will fear nothing. And if this name is written on the day of Venus, as has been said, so that by it a woman is summoned to love, let him use the art with trust, and thus he shall bring the matter[235] to accomplishment.

<The Exorcism and Uses of the Fourth Name>

§12 When you have written the fourth name, you shall exorcize it with this exorcism three times, after you have fasted and bathed once each day for three continuous days beforehand. And this name must be written with the finest saffron, musk, and aloe *raptab*, and you shall fumigate it with aloe and incense, if God wills. And this is the exorcism – you shall say: Bisam Yley Eulu^m Escelectu^m Uuaet Epyleicum Je, blessed angels of God of the whole world, amen. And these are your names: Holnuchie Egra Unct Aruaheceh Basahin Angu Uuetel Mehil Scellim L'eli Acimaleycum. With these sacred names, written in the crown of the Creator, may you send love into the heart and soul of that N., daughter of N.

<The Exorcism and Uses of the Fifth Name>

§13 This is the exorcism in which this fifth name must be exorcized after it has been written with those things necessary for it, and you shall fumigate it with the special fumigations: O God, I ask You – You are the only God, one, might, greatest, blessed, the light of heaven and earth, knowing

---

[234] The practice of keeping a written paper in a pocket (*sinus*, also means bosom or lap) during the ritual is also mentioned in *Liber Bileth* in this same codex. See Boudet, "Liber Bileth," 332; Sofer, *Solomonic Magic*, chapter 4.

[235] Here the author used *propositum*, rather than his usual *thema*.

all knowledge of secrets thoroughly, and a great exalted testimony. You remove all sorrow of the heart, and you are glorious and giver – that you may bring my matter to accomplishment, and with these spoken <names>, you will name what you wish and whomever you seek. And before this name is written, it is necessary for the practitioner to fast for one day, and to clear <the body> most cleanly in the bath, and to put on clean garments,[236] and then to enter the cleanest place. And he should be alone, and his will shall be done.

<The Exorcism of the Sixth Name>
§14 This is the exorcism of this sixth name, which you must read, and <also> over this name, after it has been written: Bis Mellah Uuebile Uueraot Uuremich'l' Uuescerafil and the blessed angels, who neither eat nor drink, since blessing is their food, and prayers are their drink. Their heads are in the heavens, and their feet touch the ends and boundaries of the earth, and their wings touch the East and the West.

<The Exorcism and Uses of the Seventh Name>
§15 And this is the exorcism of this seventh name, with which this name, after it has been written, must be exorcized. And let it be on the day of Venus: He who draws the winds from their places and the clouds from their boundaries, and who opened the sea for Moses. And He who saved Abraham, the exalted friend, and <He who is> the giver, and the honored Creator King. By these blessed, greatly exalted, most great and complete names, I ask you to bring my matter to accomplishment. This matter, however, pertains to a great thing <related> to women, which is attributed to this name of the day of Venus. And write this name with an ointment of *elgule*, that is, pearls, and *cafor*, that is, camphor, and fumigate it with *alanbar*, that is, musk, and *meuaro*, that is, rose water. And hold the sheet above the fire during the suffumigation, and afterward, let it be suspended <exposed> to the ray of the sun. And keep it with you, attached to your belt, so that neither woman nor girl, upon seeing you, can fail to immediately burn in your love. And if this name has been written on a sheet according to what has been said, with the name of a woman, she will in no way be able to resist your love.

<Preliminary Requirements and The Book of Heh'eben son of Joseph>
§16 Here is named the hour and the day according to which the triplicities of the years are divided. Therefore, whoever wishes to write any of these

---

[236] Here the author used *pannos*, rather than his usual *habitus*.

aforementioned names must first know how to devote himself to this art with all the necessary things for this teaching. And this is this book of Heh'eben, son of Joseph, the greatest sage, and through this divine knowledge he knew the day and wet years. First of all, it is necessary for you to clear <the body> in the bath for three days and abstain from carnal food. After three days, you will fumigate yourself with precious fumes and you will anoint yourself with ointments, and put on the cleanest garment, and afterward begin to write whichever of these names you wish, according to the nature of the matter, and it will be as you wish.

<General Instructions – The Second Name – Sunday>
§17 The days on which the written names are to be named. Therefore, when you wish to perform something against a king on the day of the sun and its hour, the second name must be written, and with it, the ring of the second name, and you shall exorcize it with the exorcism pertaining to it. When these things have been completed, let the sheet be fumigated with the fumigations necessary for it, as we have said above, and afterward, you will proceed as we have said. And it will be necessary for you to know the names of the triplicity and the angels, by whose order the seasons are arranged, and you must not perform anything before you know the names of the angels. And you must know the names of the wind of each triplicity and the names of the stars in various triplicities, and thus you will understand.

<General Instructions – The Third Name – Monday>
§18 The name of the day of the moon must be written for everything you wish on the day of the moon and its hour, and it is the third name. And with it, you shall exorcize its rings with its exorcism, and you shall not omit anything that belongs to it. And you must know in which triplicity you are.

<General Instructions – The Fourth Name – Tuesday>
§19 The name of the day of Mars, for the cause of war, is written with all that we have named as its own, on the day of Mars and in its hour. You must know the fourth triplicity, and the names of the angels, and stars, and winds of that triplicity, in which you will be. And write the rings of this <name> and exorcize, and having the name with you, you will not be defeated.

<General Instructions – The Fifth Name – Wednesday>
§20 The fifth name is on the day of Mercury. Therefore, whenever he wishes to discover a hidden ability, let him write the fifth name on the day of Mercury and its hour, and let him exorcize the rings and keep them with him, and through these things, he will know if an ability is hidden for someone.

<General Instructions – The Sixth Name – Thursday>

§21 The name of the day of Jupiter pertains to the chiefs and the judges, if there is any judgment in mind. And this is the sixth name, which must be written and exorcized with its rings, with you being clean in body and clothing. And let this name be written on the day of Jupiter and in its hour, and the name of the triplicity in which you are. Therefore, when you have entered the judgment, you should have this name written with you.

<General Instructions – The Seventh Name – Friday>

§22 The name of the day of Venus, for the cause of love, so that she may follow you, is written on the day of Venus and in its hour, and <with> its rings and exorcism, and determines the property of the subject, which is to be understood in all things. And you shall name the triplicity pertaining to the day and fumigate with prayers and its fumes. And with this name, let the name of the one whom you seek be written.

<On The Names of the Angels and the Triplicities>

§23 It must be said about the names of the angels who guard the seasons of the year. The blessed God called the first season spring, the second summer, the third autumn, the fourth winter, and assigned three months to each, <and> to each triplicity <He assigned> an angel, and to each angel three other assisting angels, and to each month an angel, who, in his month, serves his Lord. Therefore, it must be known that when you wish to perform something of this matter, you must recognize the triplicity in which you are, and the name of its angel, and the month, and its angel, and the name of the wind of that triplicity, and the name of its stars. Having thus calculated these things – the name of the triplicity with the names of its angels, and the name of the wind with the names of the stars – and through the great name of God, which is one of the seven names according to the aforementioned explanation, they must be sworn so that the subject may be brought to accomplishment. When these have been completed, the vow of the one seeking will be accomplished by the power of the Creator.

<The Four Triplicities>

§24 The first triplicity is from the 24th of March until the 24th of June. The second is from that day until the 24th of September. The third is from that day until the 24th of December. The fourth is from that day until the 24th of March. And this is the division of the year into four triplicities, and you will find whatever you wish concerning the names of the angels of the first triplicity.

<The Lords of the Four Triplicities>

§25 The first lord of the East is called Daniel; his ministers are named Dargimuail, Egirmail, Scagiail. The lord of the second triplicity, who presides over the West, is called Hardiail; his disciples are Gibreta Gabil, L'imisciail, Sareil. The lord of the third triplicity, who is southern, is called Anail; his companions are Farany, Uthiail, Tagilalul. The fourth lord, who is northern, is called Szadfiail; his companions are Girmichael, Himiail, Firgiail.

<The Names of the Four Winds in Each Triplicity>

§26 The wind of the East in the first triplicity is called Al'udum, in the second K'edijah, in the third Ehesrit, in the fourth the wind of the earth Mehhadi. The wind of the West in the first triplicity is Amuuueea, in the second Menbor, in the third Mehaszor, in the fourth Mamen. The wind of the South in the first triplicity Mesycur, in the second Szaramir, in the third Lak'or, in the fourth Adyrayodum. The wind of the North in the first triplicity is Tahir, in the second Aiaurmeniarobebenete, in the third K'asur Inmazdeabesze, in the fourth Gmadur.

<The Names of the Sun in Each Triplicity>

§27 The name of the sun in the first triplicity is Iebahor, in the second Aichhim, in the third Uik'alul' Szimich, in the fourth Agedhe.

<The Names of the Moon in Each Triplicity>

§28 The name of the moon in the first triplicity is Szeenisze, in the second Aichhim, in the third Iuk'al, in the fourth Gerehe.

<The Seven Angels of the Weekdays>

§29 The name of the angel of the first weekday is Rosiael, of the second Gabriael, of the third Sumuael, of the fourth Michael, of the fifth Szadsiael, of the sixth Dimuael, of the seventh K'iszsiael.

<General Instruction – The Angel of the Day>

§30 It must be known that whenever you wish to perform something, the name of the angel who guards the day on which you are must be written, with the great name of God pertaining to that day. And once the invocation of the promised names has been performed, the name of the same angel should not be omitted.

Bibliography

Abbas Ali, Hazem Hussein. "Casting Discord: An Unpublished Spell from the Egyptian National Library." In *Amulets and Talismans of the Middle East and North Africa in Context: Transmission, Efficacy and Collections*, edited by Marcela A. Garcia Probert and Petra M. Sijpesteijn, 107–125. Leiden; Boston: Brill, 2022.

Albarracín Navarro, Joaquina, and Juan Martínez Ruiz. *Medicina, farmacopea y magia en el «Misceláneo de Salomón»: texto árabe, traducción, glosas aljamiadas, estudio y glosario*. Granada: University of Granada, 1987.

Attrell, Dan, and David Porreca. *Picatrix: A Medieval Treatise on Astral Magic*. University Park: The Pennsylvania State University Press, 2019.

Barbierato, Federico. *Nella stanza dei circoli: Clavicula Salomonis e libri di magia a Venezia nei secoli XVII e XVIII*. Milan: S. Bonnard, 2002.

Baron, Solène. "Un procès de magie en Gévaudan et ses enjeux politiques (1347)." *Cahiers de Recherches Médiévales et Humanistes* 33 (2017): 385–417.

Bellusci, Alessia. "Dream Requests from the Cairo Genizah." MA Thesis, Tel Aviv University, 2011.

"Jewish Oneiric Divination: From Daniel's Prayer to the Genizah Šeʾilat Ḥalom." In *Unveiling the Hidden – Anticipating the Future: Divinatory Practices Among Jews Between Qumran and the Modern Period*, edited by Josefina Rodríguez-Arribas and Dorian Gieseler Greenbaum, 101–139. Leiden; Boston: Brill, 2021.

Berggren, J. Lennart. "Mathematics and Her Sisters in Medieval Islam: A Selective Review of Work Done from 1985 to 1995." *Historia Mathematica* 24, no. 4 (1997): 407–440.

Bohak, Gideon. *Ancient Jewish Magic: A History*. Cambridge: Cambridge University Press, 2008.

"Towards A Catalogue of The Magical, Astrological, Divinatory, and Alchemical Fragments from The Cambridge Genizah Collections." In *From a Sacred Source: Genizah Studies in Honour of Professor Stefan C. Reif*, edited by Ben Outhwaite and Siam Bhayro, 53–79. Leiden; Boston: Brill, 2011.

"Gershom Scholem and Jewish Magic." *Kabbalah: Journal for the Study of Jewish Mystical Texts* 28 (2012): 141–162. [Hebrew]

A Fifteenth-Century Manuscript of Jewish Magic. 2 vols. Los Angeles: Cherub Press, 2014.

"Babylonian Jewish Magic in Late Antiquity: Beyond the Incantation Bowls." In *Studies in Honor of Shaul Shaked*, edited by Yohanan Friedmann and Etan Kohlberg, 70–122. Jerusalem: The Israel Academy of Sciences and Humanities, 2019.

Bohak, Gideon, and Charles Burnett. *Thābit ibn Qurra "On Talismans" and Ps.-Ptolemy "On Images 1–9": together with the "Liber prestigiorum Thebidis" of Adelard of Bath*. Micrologus Library 106. Florence: SISMEL – Edizioni del Galluzzo, 2021.

Bonmariage, Cécile, and Sébastien Moureau. *Le Cercle des lettres de l'alphabet: Un traité pratique de magie des lettres attribué à Hermès*. Leiden; Boston: Brill, 2016.

Bos, Gerrit, and Charles Burnett. *Scientific Weather Forecasting in the Middle Ages*. London; New York: Routledge, 2018.

Bosworth, Clifford Edmund. "Jewish Elements in the Banū Sāsān." *Bibliotheca Orientalis* 33 (1976): 289–294.

Boudet, Jean-Patrice. *Entre science et nigromance: astrologie, divination et magie dans l'Occident médiéval (XIIe – XVe siècle)*. Paris: Publications de la Sorbonne, 2006.

"La magie au carrefour des cultures dans la Florence du Quattrocento: le "Liber Bileth" et sa démonologie." In *Penser avec les démons. Démonologues et démonologies (XIIIe-XVIIe siècles)*, edited by Martine Ostorero and Julien Véronèse, 313–345. Florence: SISMEL – Edizioni del Galluzzo, 2015.

"The Transmission of Arabic Magic in Europe (Middle Ages – Renaissance)." In *The Diffusion of The Islamic Sciences in The Western World: Conférences transculturelles de l'Union académique internationale*, edited by Agostino Paravicini Bagliani, 143–165. Firenze: SISMEL – Edizioni del Galluzzo, 2020.

Boudet, Jean-Patrice, and Julien Véronèse. "Le secret dans la magie rituelle médiévale." In *The Secret-Il Segreto*, edited by Thalia Brero and Francesco Santi, 101–150. Firenze: SISMEL – Edizioni del Galluzzo, 2006.

Boustan, Ra'anan and Joseph E. Sanzo, "Christian Magicians, Jewish Magical Idioms, and the Shared Magical Culture of Late Antiquity." *Harvard Theological Review* 110 (2017): 217–240.

Burge, Stephen R. *Angels in Islam: Jalāl al-Dīn al-Suyuṭī's al-Ḥabā'ik Fī Akhbār al-Malā'ik*. London; New York: Routledge, 2012.

Burnett, Charles. *Magic and Divination in the Middle Ages: Texts and Techniques in the Islamic and Christian Worlds*. Aldershot: Variorum, 1996.

"John of Seville and John of Spain: A Mise Au Point." *Bulletin de Philosophie Médiévale* 44 (2002): 59–78.

"Lunar Astrology: The Varieties of Texts Using Lunar Mansions, with Emphasis on Jafar Indus." In "Il sole e la luna," special issue, *Micrologus* 12 (2004): 43–133.

"Arabic Magic." In *The Routledge History of Medieval Magic*, edited by Sophie Page and Catherine Rider, 71–84. London; New York: Routledge, Taylor & Francis Group, 2019.

"Arabica Veritas: Europeans' Search for Truth in Arabic Scientific and Philosophical Literature of the Middle Ages." In *The Diffusion of the Islamic Sciences in the Western World*, edited by Agostino Paravicini Bagliani, 69–86. Firenze: SISMEL – Edizioni del Galluzzo, 2020.

"*Inscriptio Characterum*: Solomonic Magic and Paleography." In *Unveiling the Hidden—Anticipating the Future: Divinatory Practices Among Jews Between Qumran and the Modern Period*, edited by Josefina Rodríguez Arribas and Dorian Gieseler Greenbaum, 311–332. Leiden; Boston: Brill, 2021.

Burnett, Charles, and Liana Saif. "The Aping of Culinary Recipes in Magical Texts: The Case of the *Flos Naturarum* and the *Kitab al-Istijlab*." In *The Recipe from the XIIth to the XVIIth Centuries: Europe, Islam, Far East*, edited by Bruno Laurioux and Agostino Paravicini Bagliani, 117–148. Micrologus Library 116. Firenze: SISMEL – Edizioni del Galluzzo, 2023.

Canaan, Tawfiq. "The Decipherment of Arabic Talismans." In *Magic and Divination in Early Islam*, edited by Emilie Savage-Smith, 125–177. Aldershot; Burlington: Ashgate/Variorum, 2004.

Carboni, Stefano. "Gian del Kitab Al-Bulhan e scienza talismanica nel mondo Islamico." *Annali di Ca' Foscari: Rivista della Facoltà di Lingue e Letterature Straniere dell'Università di Venezia, Serie orientale*, 25, fasc. 3 (1986): 97–108.

Coullaut Cordero, Jaime. "El Kitāb Šams al-Ma'ārif al-Kubrà (al-ŷuz' al-awwal) de Aḥmad b. 'Alī al-Būnī: Sufismo y ciencias ocultas". PhD diss., Universidad de Salamanca, 2009.

Coulon, Jean-Charles. "Intégration et réception d'éléments juifs et pseudo-juifs dans la magie islamique à travers le Šams al-ma'ārif attribué à al-Būnī (m. 622/1225)". *Mélanges de l'Université Saint-Joseph* 64 (2012): 433–458.

"La magie islamique et le 'corpus bunianum' au Moyen Âge". PhD diss., Université Paris IV – Sorbonne, 2013.

La magie en terre d islam au Moyen Âge. Paris: CTHS-Histoire, 2017.

D'Agostino, Alfonso. *Astromagia: Ms. Reg. lat. 1283a*. Naples: Liguori, 1992.

de Callataÿ, Godefroid, and Sébastien Moureau, eds. *Power, Religion, and Wisdom: Orthodoxy and Heterodoxy in al-Andalus and Beyond*. Micrologus 33. Firenze: SISMEL – Edizioni del Galluzzo, 2025.

Delatte, Armand. *La catoptromancie Grecque et ses dérivés*. Liège: Vaillant-Carmann, 1932.

Dieleman, Jacco. *Priests, Tongues, and Rites: The London-Leiden Magical Manuscripts and Translation in Egyptian Ritual (100–300 CE)*. Leiden; Boston: Brill, 2005.

Dorpmüller, Sabine. *Religiöse Magie im "Buch der probaten Mittel": Analyse, kritische Edition und Übersetzung des Kitāb al-Muǧarrabāt von Muhammad ibn Yūsuf as-Sanūsī (gest. um 895/1490)*. Arabische Studien, Band 1. Wiesbaden: Harrassowitz Verlag, 2005.

Ebstein, Michael. *Mysticism and Philosophy in Al-Andalus: Ibn Masarra, Ibn al-'Arabī and the Ismaili Tradition*. Leiden; Boston: Brill, 2014.

Fahd, Toufic. *La divination arabe: études religieuses, sociologiques et folkloriques sur le milieu natif de l'Islam*. Leiden: Brill, 1966.

Fanger, Claire. "Plundering the Egyptian Treasure: John the Monk's *Book of Visions* and Its Relation to the *Ars Notoria* of Solomon." In *Conjuring Spirits: Texts and Traditions of Medieval Ritual Magic*, edited by Claire Fanger, 216–249. University Park: Penn State University Press, 1998.

Fodor, Alexander. "An Arabic Version of 'Sefer ha-Razim'." *Jewish Studies Quarterly* 13 (2006): 412–427.

———. "An Arabic Version of 'The Sword of Moses.'" In *Continuity and Innovation in the Magical Tradition*, edited by Gideon Bohak, Yuval Harari, and Shaul Shaked, 341–386. Leiden; Boston: Brill, 2011.

Foucault, Michel. "What Is an Author?" In *Aesthetics, Method, and Epistemology*, edited by James D. Faubion, 205–222. New York: New Press, 1998

Garcia Probert, Marcela A., and Petra M. Sijpesteijn, eds. *Amulets and Talismans of the Middle East and North Africa in Context: Transmission, Efficacy and Collections*. Leiden; Boston: Brill, 2022.

Gardiner, Noah. "Forbidden Knowledge? Notes on the Production, Transmission, and Reception of the Major Works of Aḥmad al-Būnī." *Journal of Arabic and Islamic Studies* 12 (2012): 81–143.

———. "Esotericism in a Manuscript Culture: Aḥmad al-Būnī and His Readers through the Mamlūk Period." PhD diss., University of Michigan, 2014.

Gehr, Damaris. "'Gaudent brevitatem moderni': rielaborazioni della teoria magica nel tardo medioevo Sull'esempio dell'Almandal di Salomone". *Società e Storia* 139 (2013): 1–36.

——. "Beringarius Ganellus and the *Summa Sacre Magice*: Magic as the Promotion of God's Kingship." In *The Routledge History of Medieval Magic*, edited by Sophie Page and Catherine Rider, 237–253. Routledge Histories. London; New York: Routledge, Taylor & Francis Group, 2019.

Gentile, Sebastiano, and Carlos Gilly. *Marsilio Ficino e il ritorno di Ermete Trismegisto*. Firenze: Centro Di, 1999.

Goldziher, Ignaz. "The Sabbath Institution in Islam." In *The Development of Islamic Ritual*, edited by Gerald Hawting, 33–47. Aldershot; Burlington: Ashgate/Variorum, 2006.

Hamès, Constant. "Maṇḍalas et sceaux talismaniques musulmans". In De l'Arabie à l'Himalaya. Chemins croisés: en hommage à Marc Gaborieau, edited by Véronique Bouillier and Catherine Servan Schreiber, 145–159. Paris: Maisonneuve & Larose, 2004.

Harari, Yuval. *Jewish Magic before the Rise of Kabbalah*. Detroit: Wayne State University Press, 2017.

Hasse, Dag Nikolaus. *Success and Suppression: Arabic Sciences and Philosophy in the Renaissance*. Cambridge; London: Harvard University Press, 2016.

Huss, Boaz. *Mystifying Kabbalah: Academic Scholarship, National Theology, and New Age Spirituality*. New York: Oxford University Press, 2020.

Ibn Khaldūn. *The Muqaddimah. An Introduction to History*. Translated by Franz Rosenthal. Princeton: Princeton University Press, 1958.

Idel, Moshe. "The Concept of the Torah in Heikhalot Literature and Its Reverberations in Kabbalah." *Jerusalem Studies in Jewish Thought* 1 (1982): 23–84. [Hebrew]

Jawbarī, ʿAbd al-Raḥmān ibn ʿUmar. *The Book of Charlatans*. Edited by Manuela Dengler. Translated by Humphrey T. Davies. New York: New York University Press, 2020.

Kieckhefer, Richard. *Forbidden Rites: A Necromancer's Manual of the Fifteenth Century*. University Park: Pennsylvania State University Press, 1998.

Klaassen, Frank. *The Transformations of Magic: Illicit Learned Magic in the Later Middle Ages and Renaissance*. University Park: Pennsylvania State University Press, 2013.

Leicht, Reimund. *Astrologumena Judaica: Untersuchungen zur Geschichte der astrologischen Literatur der Juden*. Tübingen: Mohr Siebeck, 2006.

Lev, Efraim, and Zohar Amar. *Practical Materia Medica of the Medieval Eastern Mediterranean According to the Cairo Genizah*. Leiden; Boston: Brill, 2008.

Lucentini, Paolo, and Vittoria Perrone Compagni. *I testi e i codici di Ermete nel Medioevo*. Firenze: Polistampa, 2001.

Macler, Frédéric. *L'enluminure arménienne profane*. Paris: P. Geuthner, 1928.

Mallett, Alex, Catherine Rider, and Dionisius A. Agius, eds. *Magic in Malta: Sellem Bin al-Sheikh Mansur and the Roman Inquisition, 1605*. Leiden; Boston: Brill, 2022.

Martin, Ruth. *Witchcraft and the Inquisition in Venice, 1550–1650*. Oxford; New York: Blackwell, 1989.

McCluskey, Stephen C. *Astronomies and Cultures in Early Medieval Europe*. Cambridge: Cambridge University Press, 1997.

Melvin-Koushki, Matthew S. "Magic in Islam between Religion and Science." *Magic, Ritual, and Witchcraft* 14 (2019): 255–287.

Melvin-Koushki, Matthew S., and Noah Gardiner, eds. "Islamicate Occultism: New Perspectives." Special issue, *Arabica* 64 (2017).

Newman, William. "New Light on the Identity of 'Geber.'" *Sudhoffs Archiv* 69, no. 1 (1985): 76–90.

The Summa Perfectionis of Pseudo-Geber: A Critical Edition, Translation and Study. Leiden; New York: Brill, 1991.

Nünlist, Tobias. *Dämonenglaube im Islam: Eine Untersuchung unter besonderer Berücksichtigung schriftlicher Quellen aus der vormodernen Zeit (600–1500)*. Boston: De Gruyter, 2015.

Ockenström, Lauri. "The Deviance of Toz: The Reception of Toz Graecus and Magical Works Attributed to Toz in the Twelfth and Thirteenth Centuries." In *Esotericism and Deviance*, edited by Manon Hedenborg White and Tim Rudbøg, 129–154. Leiden; Boston: Brill, 2023.

Ockenström, Lauri, and Vajra Regan. "The Hermetic Origins of the *Liber Sigillorum* of Techel." *The Journal of Medieval Latin* 33 (2023): 173–266.

Page, Sophie. "Magic and the Pursuit of Wisdom: The 'Familiar' Spirit in the Liber Theysolius." *La Corónica: A Journal of Medieval Hispanic Languages, Literatures, and Cultures* 36, no. 1 (2007): 41–70.

"Uplifting Souls: The *Liber de Essentia Spirituum* and the *Liber Razielis*." In *Invoking Angels: Theurgic Ideas and Practices, Thirteenth* to Sixteenth Centuries, edited by Claire Fanger, 79–112. University Park: Pennsylvania State University Press, 2012.

Perrone Compagni, Vittoria. "Studiosus incantationibus: Adelardo di Bath, Ermete e Thabit." *Giornale critico della filosofia italiana* 21 (2001): 36–61.

Pick, Lucy K. *Conflict and Coexistence: Archbishop Rodrigo and the Muslims and Jews in Medieval Spain*. Ann Arbor: University of Michigan, 2004.

Pingree, David. "The Diffusion of Arabic Magical Texts in Western Europe." In *La diffusione delle scienze islamiche nel medio evo europeo*, edited by B. Scarcia Amoretti, 57–102. Rome: Accademia Nazionale dei Lincei, 1987.

"Al-Ṭabarī On The Prayers to The Planets." *Bulletin d'études orientales* 44 (1992): 105–117.

"Learned Magic in the Time of Frederick II." *Micrologus* 2 (1994): 39–56.

Porat, Oded. *Brit ha-Menuḥa*. Jerusalem: Magnes Press, 2016. [Hebrew]

Porter, Venetia, Liana Saif, and Emilie Savage-Smith. "Medieval Islamic Amulets, Talismans, and Magic." In *A Companion to Islamic Art and Architecture*, edited by Finbarr Barry Flood and Gülru Necipoğlu, 1: 521–557. New Jersey: Wiley, 2017.

Principe, Lawrence. *The Secrets of Alchemy*. Chicago: University of Chicago Press, 2013.

Regan, Vajra. "The *De consecratione lapidum*: A Previously Unknown Thirteenth-Century Version of the *Liber Almandal Salomonis*, Newly Introduced with a Critical Edition and Translation." *The Journal of Medieval Latin* 28 (2018): 277–333.

Regourd, Anne. "Images de djinns et exorcisme dans le *Mandal al-sulaymānī*". In *Images et magie: Picatrix entre Orient et Occident*, edited by Jean-Patrice Boudet, Anna Caiozzo, and Nicolas Weill-Parot, 253–294. Paris: H. Champion, 2011.

"*Al-mandal al-sulaymānī* appliqué: une section interpolée dans le ms. Sanaa 2774". *The Arabist: Budapest Studies in Arabic* 37 (2016): 135–151.

"A Twentieth-Century Manuscript of the *Kitāb al-Mandal al-Sulaymānī* (IES Ar. 286, Addis Ababa, Ethiopia): Texts on Practices & Texts in Practices." In *Amulets and Talismans of the Middle East and North Africa in Context: Transmission, Efficacy and Collections*, edited by Marcela A. Garcia Probert and Petra M. Sijpesteijn, 47–77. Leiden; Boston: Brill, 2022.

Saar, Ortal-Paz. *Jewish Love Magic: From Late Antiquity to the Middle Ages*. Leiden; Boston: Brill, 2017.

Saif, Liana. *The Arabic Influences on Early Modern Occult Philosophy*. Basingstoke: Palgrave Macmillan, 2015.

——— "The Cows and the Bees: Arabic Sources and Parallels for Pseudo-Plato's *Liber Vaccae*." *Journal of the Warburg and Courtauld Institutes* 79 (2016): 1–47.

Saif, Liana, Francesca Leoni, Matthew Melvin-Koushki, and Farouk Yahya, eds. *Islamicate Occult Sciences in Theory and Practice*. Leiden; Boston: Brill, 2021.

Saliba, George. *Islamic Science and the Making of the European Renaissance*. Cambridge: MIT Press, 2014.

Salzer, Dorothea M. *Die Magie der Anspielung: Form und Funktion der biblischen Anspielungen in den magischen Texten der Kairoer Geniza*. Tübingen: Mohr Siebeck, 2010.

Samsó, Julio. "Lunar Mansions and Timekeeping in Western Islam." *Suhayl* 8 (2008): 121–161.

Savage-Smith, Emilie, ed. *Magic and Divination in Early Islam*. Aldershot; Burlington: Ashgate/Variorum, 2004.

Schäfer, Peter, und Shaul Shaked. *Magische Texte aus der Kairoer Geniza*. 3 Bde. Tübingen: Mohr Siebeck, 1994–1999.

Scholem, Gershom. "An Inquiry in the Kabbala of R. Isaac Ben Jacob Hacohen: III. R. Moses of Burgos, the Disciple of R. Isaac." *Tarbitz* 3, no. 3 (1932): 258–86. [Hebrew]

——— "Some Sources of Jewish-Arabic Demonology." *Journal of Jewish Studies* 16 (1965): 1–13. [Hebrew]

——— "Bilar (Bilad, Bilid, BEΛIAP), the King of the Demons." In *Demons, Spirits and Souls*, edited by Esther Liebes, 9–51. Jerusalem: Yad Ben Zvi, 2004. [Hebrew]

Selove, Emily. *The Donkey King: Asinine Symbology in Ancient and Medieval Magic*. Cambridge: Cambridge University Press, 2023.

Shaked, Shaul. "On Jewish Literature of Magic in Muslim Countries: Comments and Specimens." *Peamim* 15 (1983): 15–28. [Hebrew]

Siraisi, Nancy G. *Avicenna in Renaissance Italy: The Canon and Medical Teaching in Italian Universities after 1500*. Princeton: Princeton University Press, 1987.

Sofer, Gal. "The Hebrew Manuscripts of Mafte'ah Shelomoh and an Inquiry into the Magic of the Sabbateans." *Kabbalah: Journal for the Study of Jewish Mystical Texts* 32 (2014): 135–174. [Hebrew]

"Wearing God, Consecrating Body Parts: Berengar Ganell's *Summa Sacre Magice* and Shi'ur Qomah." *Magic, Ritual, and Witchcraft* 16, no. 3 (2021): 304–334.

"Hebrew 'Solomonic Magic': The Case of the *Ydea Salomonis*." In *Magic and Language: Perspectives on Jewish and Christian Magic in Early Modern Europe*, edited by Yuval Harari, Gerold Necker, and Marco Frenschkowski, 153–187. Wiesbaden: Harrassowitz Verlag, 2024.

"The Great Name: An Unknown Genizah-Fragment of Sefer HaRazim's Tradition and Its Latin Recension." *Ginzei Qedem* 20 (2024): 75–107. [Hebrew]

Solomonic Magic: Methodology, Texts, and Histories. Leiden; Boston: Brill, 2025.

"Upon the Magician's Escritoire: A Recently Discovered Hebrew *Clavicula Salomonis*." *Harvard Theological Review* [in press].

Strickland, Debra Higgs. *Saracens, Demons, and Jews: Making Monsters in Medieval Art*. Princeton: Princeton University Press, 2003.

Stroumsa, Sarah. "Twelfth Century Concepts of Soul and Body: The Maimonidean Controversy in Baghdad." In *Self, Soul and Body in Religious Experience*, edited by Albert I. Baumgartner, Guy Stroumsa, and Jan Assmann, 313–334. Leiden; Boston; Köln: Brill, 1998.

Suárez de la Torre, Emilio. "Pseudepigraphy and Magic." In *Fakes and Forgers of Classical Literature: Ergo Decipiatur!*, edited by Javier Martínez, 243–262. Leiden; Boston: Brill, 2014.

Thorndike, Lynn. *A History of Magic and Experimental Science*. 8 vols. New York; London: Columbia University Press, 1923–1958.

"Traditional Medieval Tracts Concerning Engraved Astrological Images." In *Mélanges Auguste Pelzer: Etudes d'histoire littéraire et doctrinale de la Scolastique médiévale offertes à Monseigneur Auguste Pelzer*, 217–273. Leuven: Bibliothèque de l'Université, 1947.

Tolan, John Victor. *Saracens: Islam in the Medieval European Imagination*. New York: Columbia University Press, 2002.

Torijano, Pablo. *Solomon, the Esoteric King: From King to Magus, Development of a Tradition*. Leiden; Boston: Brill, 2002.

Vajda, Georges. "Sur quelques éléments juifs et pseudo-juifs dans l'encyclopédie magique de Bûnî." In *Ignace Goldziher Memorial Volume*, edited by Samuel Löwinger and Joseph Somogyi, 1:387–392. Budapest: Globus, 1948.

Veenstra, Jan R. "The Holy Almandal: Angels and The Intellectual Aims of Magic." In *The Metamorphosis of Magic from Late Antiquity to the*

Early Modern Period, edited by Jan N. Bremmer and Jan R. Veenstra, 189–229. Leuven: Peeters, 2002.

"Honorius and the Sigil of God: The *Liber Iuratus* in Berengario Ganell's *Summa Sacre Magice*." In *Invoking Angels: Theurgic Ideas and Practices, Thirteenth to Sixteenth Centuries*, edited by Claire Fanger, 151–191. University Park: Pennsylvania State University Press, 2012.

Véronèse, Julien. "La transmission groupée des textes de magie salomonienne de l'Antiquité au Moyen âge: bilan historiographique, inconnues et pistes de recherche." In *L'antiquité tardive dans les collections médiévales*, 193–223. Rome: École Française de Rome, 2008.

L'Almandal et l'Almadel latins au Moyen Âge: introduction et éditions critiques. Firenze: SISMEL edizioni del Galluzzo, 2012.

Weill-Parot, Nicolas. *Les "images astrologiques" au Moyen Âge et à la Renaissance: spéculations intellectuelles et pratiques magiques (XIIe-XVe siècle)*. Paris: Honoré Champion, 2002.

"Cecco D'ascoli and Antonio Da Montolmo: The Building of a 'Nigromantical' Cosmology and the Birth of the Author-Magician." In *The Routledge History of Medieval Magic*, edited by Sophie Page and Catherine Rider, 225–236. London; New York: Routledge, Taylor & Francis Group, 2019.

Winkler, Hans Alexander. *Siegel und Charaktere in der mohammedanischen Zauberei*. Berlin; Leipzig: Walter De Gruyter & Co, 1930.

Worrell, William H. "Ink, Oil and Mirror Gazing Ceremonies in Modern Egypt." *Journal of the American Oriental Society* 36 (1916): 37–53.

Zadeh, Travis. "Postscript: Cutting Ariadne's Thread, or How to Think Otherwise in the Maze." In *Islamicate Occult Sciences in Theory and Practice*, edited by Liana Saif, Francesca Leoni, Matthew S. Melvin-Koushki, and Farouk Yahya, 607–650. Leiden; Boston: Brill, 2021.

"Tracing the Sorcerer's Circle: Demons, Polysemy, and the Boundaries of Islamic Normativity." In *Power, Religion, and Wisdom: Orthodoxy and Heterodoxy in al-Andalus and Beyond*, edited by Godefroid de Callataÿ and Sébastien Moureau, 91–154. Micrologus 33. Firenze: SISMEL – Edizioni del Galluzzo, 2025.

Zsom, Dora. "Another Arabic Version of *Sefer ha-Razim* and *Ḥarba de-Moše*: A New Sifr Ādam Manuscript." *The Arabist: Budapest Studies in Arabic* 37 (2016): 179–201.

"A Judeo-Arabic Fragment of the Magical Treatise *Kitāb Dāʾirat al-Aḥruf al-Abğadiyya*." *The Arabist: Budapest Studies in Arabic* 38 (2017): 95–120.

Cambridge Elements

Magic

William Pooley
University of Bristol

William Pooley is Senior Lecturer in Modern History at the University of Bristol and co-editor of the forthcoming *Cambridge Companion to the Witch*. He is the author of *Body and Tradition in Nineteenth-century France: Félix Arnaudin and the Moorlands of Gascony* (2019) and co-author of the CUP Element *Creative Histories of Witchcraft: France, 1790–1940* (2022). His next book is a history of witchcraft in France from the French Revolution to World War Two.

About the Series

Elements in Magic aims to restore the study of magic, broadly defined, to a central place within culture: one which it occupied for many centuries before being set apart by changing discourses of rationality and meaning. Understood as a continuing and potent force within global civilisation, magical thinking is imaginatively approached here as a cluster of activities, attitudes, beliefs and motivations which include topics such as alchemy, astrology, divination, exorcism, the fantastical, folklore, haunting, supernatural creatures, necromancy, ritual, spirit possession and witchcraft.

Cambridge Elements

Magic

Elements in the Series

The War on Witchcraft: Andrew Dickson White, George Lincoln Burr, and the Origins of Witchcraft Historiography
Jan Machielsen

Witchcraft and the Modern Roman Catholic Church
Francis Young

'Ritual Litter' Redressed
Ceri Houlbrook

Representing Magic in Modern Ireland: Belief, History, Culture
Andrew Sneddon

Creative Histories of Witchcraft: France, 1790–1940
Poppy Corbett, Anna Kisby Compton and William G. Pooley

Witchcraft and Paganism in Midcentury Women's Detective Fiction
Jem Bloomfield

The Gut
Elizabeth Pérez

The Donkey King
Emily Selove

Amulets in Magical Practice
Jay Johnston

Staging Witchcraft before the Law: Skepticism, Performance as Proof, and Law as Magic in Early Modern Witch Trials
Julie Stone Peters

Lowcountry Conjure Magic: Historical Archaeology on a Plantation Slave Quarter
Sharon K. Moses

Conjuring the Arab Magician: Intercultural Histories of Magic
Gal Sofer

A full series listing is available at: www.cambridge.org/EMGI

For EU product safety concerns, contact us at Calle de José Abascal, 56–1°, 28003 Madrid, Spain or eugpsr@cambridge.org.

www.ingramcontent.com/pod-product-compliance
Lightning Source LLC
LaVergne TN
LVHW011852060526
838200LV00054B/4292